MAKING MUSIC WITH iSCORE:
SUPPORT MATERIALS FOR TEACHERS

MAKING MUSIC WITH iSCORE:

SUPPORT MATERIALS FOR TEACHERS

Julia Brook
Rena Upitis
Elaine Lau
Joseph Ferretti
Heidi Saario
Julia Fountain
Jodie Compeau
Anne Wade
Einat Idan

Second edition September 2013

Wintergreen Studios Press
Township of South Frontenac, PO Box 75, Yarker, ON, Canada K0K 3N0

Copyright © 2013 by Rena Upitis. All rights reserved under the International and Pan-American Copyright Conventions. No part of this book may be reproduced in any form or by electronic or mechanical means, including information storage and retrieval systems, without permission in writing from the publisher, except by a reviewer, who may quote brief passages in a review. The views expressed in this work are those of the author and do not necessarily reflect those of the publisher.

Every effort has been made to contact the copyright holders, artists, photographers, and authors whose work appears in this text for permission to reprint material. We regret any oversights and we will be happy to rectify them in future editions.

>Book and cover design by Rena Upitis
>Composed in Candara and Arial, typefaces designed by Monotype Typography.

Library and Archives Canada Cataloguing in Publication
Brook, Julia. 1975–
Making Music with iSCORE: Support Materials for Teachers/Julia Brook

ISBN-13: 978-0991872206   ISBN-10: 0991872207
1. Education—General.

>I.   Title. Making Music with iSCORE: Support Materials for Teachers
>Legal Deposit—Library and Archives Canada

TABLE OF CONTENTS

INTRODUCTION 1
   Developing Independent Musicians with iSCORE 3
   What is Our Current Teaching Context? 4
   What Does the Research Tell Us? 5
      Music Practising—What Happens at Home? 6
      Self-Regulated Learning Theory: Key Points 8
         Why is Self-Regulated Learning Important? 9
         What is the Self-Regulated Learning Cycle? 10
   More about iSCORE and electronic portfolio tools 12
   And so … delve in! 14

QUICK REFERENCE GUIDES 17
   Choosing Your Settings 19
   Notes & Posts 21
      To Get to Another Home Page 22
      Leaving a Post on Someone's Home Page 23
      Other Important Notes & Posts Features 24
   Finding and Pasting Links 25
   Using the Annotator 27
      Uploading Media into Your *Teacher* Portfolio 27
      Uploading Media into Your *Student's* Portfolio 28
      Adding an Annotation to a Video/Audio Recording 28
      Adding a Text Annotation 29
      Adding a Recorded Annotation 29
   Using The Calendar 30
      Creating Categories in Your Calendar 31
      Creating and Sharing Events in Your Calendar 32
   Using iSCORE Files 34
      Uploading Resources to Your Files Tab 34
      Viewing and Sorting Your Files 35
      To Add a File 36
      To Add a Link 36
      Sharing Your Files 37

DETAILED USER GUIDE 39
   iSCORE Manage 41
      My Classes 41

  Link/Unlink Classes 44
  Pending Requests 45
  My Students 46
  Invite Students 46
  Students Requesting to Join Your Class 47
  Teacher Tags 49

Home 50

  Settings 51
  General Goals 52
  To Do List 53
  Notes & Posts 54
  To Write on Someone Else's Notes & Posts 55
  Notifications 55
  Upcoming Events 55

Planning 56

  Labels 56
  Task Description 57
  Criteria 57
  Goals 58
  Strategies 59
  General Goal Connections 60
  Tags 61
  Schedule 62
  Motivation 62
  Saving 62

Doing 63

  Text Editor 63
  Audio Recorder 64
  Attach a File 65
  Paste a Link 65
  Uploading Media into Your *Teacher* Portfolio 66
  Uploading Media into Your *Student's* Portfolio 66
  Adding an Annotation to a Video/Audio Recording 66
  Adding a Text Annotation 67
  Adding a Recorded Annotation 68
  Connect to Other Software 68
  My Plan 69
  Checklist 69
  Timer 69
  Journal 70
  Progress 70

Reflecting 71

  Self-Evaluation 71

  Cause 72
  Satisfaction 72
  Lessons Learned 72
  Saved Filters 73

Overview 74
Calendar 75
  Creating Categories in Your Calendar 76
  Creating and Sharing Events in Your Calendar 77

Files 78
  To Add a File 78
  To Add a Link 78
  Searching Your Files 79
  Sharing Your Files 79

Sharing 81
  Viewing Student Portfolios from Sharing 82

Mailbox 83

iSCORE iDEAS 85
Using the iSCORE Home Page as an Online Dictation Book 87
Using iSCORE to Compare Performances 89
Using iSCORE to Compose 90
  Five ways to use iSCORE to improvise and compose 90
  OK, so how do they get started? 91
  Couldn't students just start by doing? 92

Using iSCORE to Practise 93
  Planning 93
  Doing 96
  Reflecting 97

Using iSCORE to Help With Ear Training 100
Using iSCORE for Student Communication 102
Encouraging Communication Between Students and Parents: A Guide for Teachers to Share with Parents 104

STUDENT EXEMPLARS 107
The Home Page 109
Work: Planning, Doing, & Reflecting 111
  Using iSCORE to Learn a Piece: *Mouse in the Coal Bin* 112
  Using iSCORE to Learn a Piece: *Prelude in B minor* 114
  Using iSCORE to Learn a Piece by Ear: *The Scientist* 118
  Using iSCORE to Compose: *Crescent* 120
  Using iSCORE for a Quick Study: *Bagatelle* 122

ACKNOWLEDGEMENTS 129

INTRODUCTION

Developing Independent Musicians with iSCORE

iSCORE is a digital learning portfolio that was developed to help students make the journey to becoming self-regulating, independent musicians. This is not a journey that students undertake alone. The students who are most likely to become joyful and independent musicians also rely on the support and guidance of parents, teachers, and fellow students. iSCORE is a tool that integrates the contributions of parents, teachers, and students, creating a living portfolio for documenting progress and reflecting on learning, and providing many ways of planning and approaching new challenges.

iSCORE is a web-based practice and communication tool. It is designed to help motivate students to take responsibility for their practising and overall music learning and music creation. iSCORE supports students as they learn to set realistic goals, create new work, edit and share their work, and respond to feedback from teachers, peers, parents, and other musicians. iSCORE also enables teachers to communicate with their students during the week, so that practising between lessons becomes more focussed and successful. One of the key features of iSCORE is the annotation tool, which allows teachers, parents, and students to comment on video and audio recordings. iSCORE also capitalizes on 21st century learners' propensity for using technology. The web-based nature of the tool provides flexibility, allowing users to access the tool from any computer.

This manual is designed for you, the teacher who is using iSCORE in your music-teaching studio. You will learn about iSCORE by by trying the activities and approaches that we describe. You can also learn about iSCORE by using online support materials, which include examples of portfolios (www.iscorenews.com), by working with your students as they explore iSCORE, by interacting with other teachers, and by learning from the Royal Conservatory (RCM) teacher advisors. Welcome to iSCORE!

What is Our Current Teaching Context?

While millions of children take weekly lessons and yearly conservatory examinations in countries worldwide, many students stop taking lessons after a year or two (McPherson, Davidson, & Faulkner, 2012). Indeed, some students stop playing only weeks after their lessons begin, when they realize the level of commitment that is required to learn to play an instrument so that it is personally satisfying (McPherson, Davidson, & Faulkner, 2012).

This lack of engagement may result, in part, from the isolation that music students experience when expected to practise at home between weekly lessons. A recent survey of Canadian studio teachers indicated that an overwhelming majority of teachers also experience a sense of professional isolation (Feldman, 2010).

But the lack of engagement may also be a result of students not being given enough freedom and support to direct their own learning, to choose repertoire, and to engage in practices of composition and improvisation. To be sure, there are some independent music teachers who engage in all of these practices, and with great success. But other teachers fall into the pattern of teaching as they were taught—which may not be the most effective form of teaching in today's world.

Technology can reduce isolation for both music students and their teachers by providing the means for students and teachers to interact between weekly lessons. One of the reasons we developed iSCORE was to provide a tool to reduce the professional isolation experienced by teachers. But our main reason for developing iSCORE was to support the transformation of music studio teaching and learning.

What Does the Research Tell Us?

Studio instruction refers to one-on-one instruction in home-based or music school studios, where students take weekly 30- to 60-minute lessons from independent music teachers. The approach taken in studio instruction is traditionally in the form of a master-apprentice dyad: the student studies under the tutelage of an expert musician who has been trained in performance and/or pedagogy (Kennell, 2002).

Research shows that student learning can be more enduring if students take greater control over their own learning processes, and in so

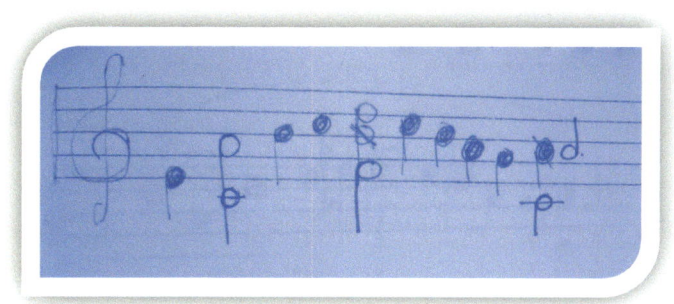

doing, become self-regulated learners over time (Abrami, Venkatesh, Meyer, & Wade, in press). We believe that iSCORE can help students become independent earlier in their musical studies, since it includes specific features for supporting student self-regulation. We also hold the view that a shift from the master-apprentice model to a co-regulation model of learning will help students remain engaged with the process of learning to sing or play an instrument, so that they not only remain motivated, but also develop ways of practising regularly and effectively.

Music Practising—What Happens at Home?

Research suggests that it takes approximately 16 years to attain international levels of achievement (Hallam, 2012) and that even moderate levels of achievement require considerable practice time and sustained commitment (Hallam, 1995; Hallam & Bautista, 2012). Further, during the practising between lessons that is required to learn to sing or to play a musical instrument, the student, often alone, must apply the ideas presented at the lesson to improve his or her skills. This is a tall order: students must plan, implement, and reflect on their progress and create subsequent plans or change their original plan to respond to their progress or lack thereof during the practice session.

Evidence suggests that advanced musicians focus on aspects of their playing that can be improved and seek help from others when facing technical difficulties (McPherson & Zimmerman, 2011).

Novice players typically play or sing their repertoire repeatedly without identifying errors or focusing on difficult passages. They also have difficulty selecting appropriate practice strategies in general (Hallam, 2012; Hallam & Bautista, 2012; McPherson & Renwick, 2001). Both the amount of time spent practising and types of practice activities are predictors of success (Barry & Hallam, 2002; Zhukov, 2009). Hallam (2012) shows how better performance and more joyful engagement with music in general comes from deliberate practising, which involves identifying goals, receiving meaningful feedback through a supportive social network, and having opportunities for mindful repetition.

While teachers often discuss practice strategies with students during their lessons, the research shows that very few students apply these strategies in their practice sessions when they are working on their instrument alone (Barry & Hallam, 2002; McPherson & Renwick, 2011). This is surely not a surprise to most independent music teachers! But why do students fail to apply strategies they have been taught? This lack of application could be due to a lack of interest in practising in general. But it could also result from a lack of experience in teaching oneself, pointing to the need to have other supports to help one plan, execute one's plan, and reflect on one's musical learning.

Self-Regulated Learning Theory: Key Points

Self-regulation is the development of a set of constructive thoughts, feelings, and behaviours that affect one's learning. Learning processes are planned and adapted to support the achievement of personal goals as the learning environment constantly changes.

Self-regulated learning (SRL) has been identified as a feature of deliberate music practice (Bartolome, 2009; McPherson & Renwick, 2011; Miksza, 2007), and it is widely recognized as a core aspect of metacognition (McPherson & Zimmerman, 2011; Zimmerman & Schunk, 2011). SRL research has been conducted in four broad domains: (a) metacognitive and cognitive, (b) social and motivational, (c) behavioural and cognitive, and (d) developmental (Zimmerman & Schunk, 2011). Meta-analyses of research on SRL indicate that motivation is a key ingredient in SRL intervention programs and its inclusion can result in improved academic performance (Dignath, Buettner, & Langfeldt, 2008).

McPherson, Davidson, and Faulkner (2012) have suggested that self-regulation may not be the only aspect of successful music practising. They posit that *co-regulation*, a combination of self-regulation and various forms of external regulation, such as the support provided by music teachers, is necessary to support music learning. External regulation could also include support from parents and peers. McPherson, Davidson, and Faulkner (2012) followed 157 students in Australia over a 14-year period, and found that having supportive parents, a variety of performance opportunities, and positive peer interactions served to enhance student learning. Further, their results highlighted the importance of playful practising; students were engaged more deeply when they were provided with opportunities to explore sounds in supportive learning environments.

Why is Self-Regulated Learning Important?

Learners with high levels of self-regulation have control over the attainment of their goals. They can focus on the process of how to attain these goals and gain ownership over their learning. Ultimately, self-regulation skills and processes ensure that students become lifelong learners.

What is the Self-Regulated Learning Cycle?

Occasionally, plunging into a task and getting through it as well as one can, is a good way to approach a creative endeavour. Other times, a deliberate approach involving planning, doing, and reflecting is more effective.

The self-regulated learning cycle requires the learner to prepare for the learning process by: setting goals that are realistic and valuable; making concrete plans to achieve them; and assessing the degree of motivation and effort needed to invest in the task.

Once this tentative "roadmap" is sketched out, the learner tackles the task. At this stage, it is important to monitor progress and make sure the plan that was put in place is, in fact, effective in bringing the goal closer. If it isn't, the learner can make the necessary changes that will help steer him or her towards the desired goal.

When the task has been completed, reflection on the outcome and the learning process are critical for further growth. Learners are encouraged to evaluate themselves and to explain the outcomes as the result of an ever-improving process, rather than in terms of static, innate capabilities.

The cyclical nature of this process is as important as any of its stages. Using strategies that have worked best in certain situations, or adjusting a goal to make it more realistic, are just two of the ways in which a learner can adjust his or her learning process. As the learner makes modifications and reflects on their outcomes, a learning process evolves that is uniquely suited to him or her.

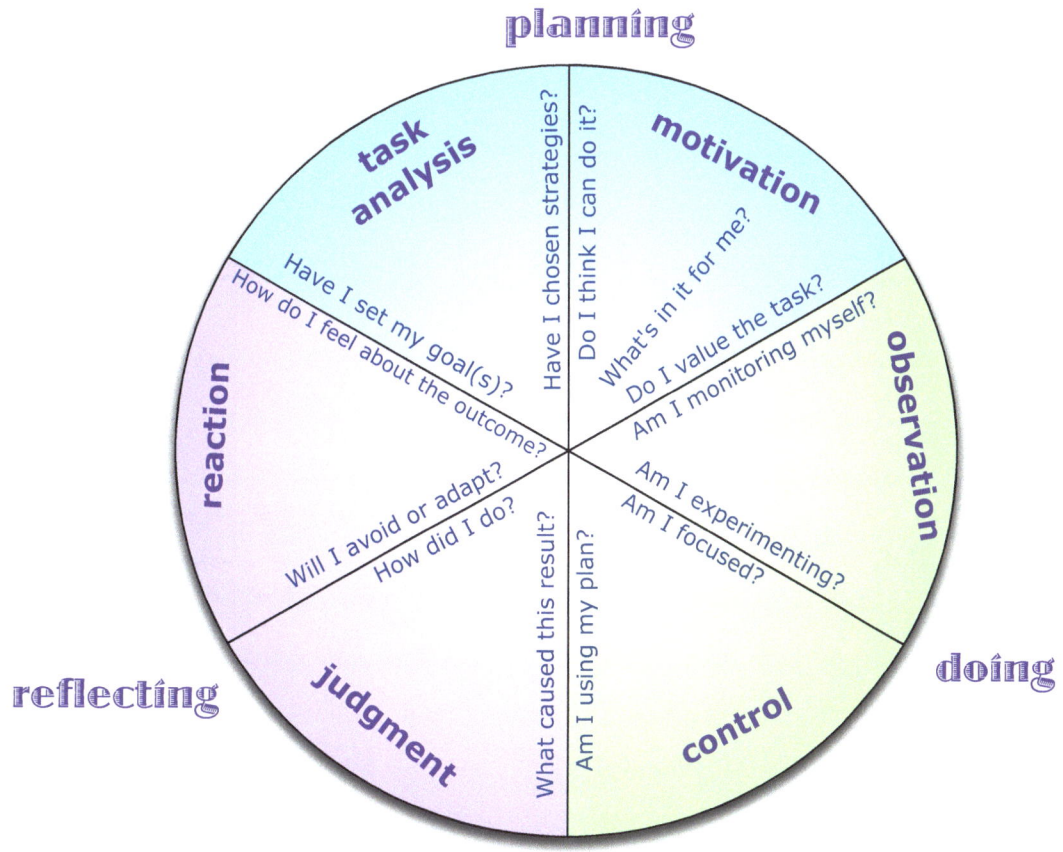

Most music teachers are aware that self-regulation can and should be taught to music students. While keeping track of all the components of self-regulated learning may seem like a daunting task to a busy teacher, it is reassuring to know that iSCORE has all the relevant steps already embedded in it. When creating a work in iSCORE, the learner will be encouraged to perform various planning, doing and reflecting tasks. At the same time, they are not *obligated* to do any of them. The software is built in a drill-down fashion: if the learner or teacher would like to concentrate more on a particular aspect of self-regulation, he or she can do so by exploring all the support that iSCORE has to offer on the SRL process. However, if teachers or students do not wish to work so extensively on one part, they can simply use the aspects of the tool that are most relevant to the task at hand.

More about iSCORE and electronic portfolio tools

Electronic portfolios are used to store and organize digital content and may be used in a number of ways—to archive work, to showcase work, and also, to support the learning process (Abrami & Barrett, 2005). When students use *learning portfolios*, they often assume more responsibility for their work and come to understand their strengths and limitations (Zellers & Mudrey, 2007). In addition to developing self-regulated learning skills, students may also achieve greater learning gains (Abrami, Venkatesh, Meyer, & Wade, in press). iSCORE embodies the principles of self-regulated learning, with places to plan, execute one's plan, and reflect on one's learning. iSCORE is therefore a learning portfolio, as well as a place to archive progress and musical achievements.

There are three pages in iSCORE that support learning (Home, Work, Overview) and four pages that facilitate communication between teachers and students (Sharing, Calendar, Files, Mailbox). Together, these features support students' growth as self-regulated learners. The diagram shows how each of the planning, doing, and reflecting phases are captured by iSCORE's features in the "work" section of iSCORE—the heart of the tool.

Studies have demonstrated that iSCORE, and its predecessor, ePEARL, enhance musical competencies and encourage teachers to use self-regulation strategies to guide student learning (Brook, Troop, & Upitis, 2011; Upitis, Abrami, Brook, Troop, & Catalano, 2010). Because the iSCORE platform allows students to share their portfolios with teachers, parents, and peers, students can upload work produced elsewhere or use the embedded recorder and text features to create work directly in the portfolio for others to see. These features have been found to be highly motivating for students. The social media features of iSCORE have also been found to be motivating for students and teachers alike. Teachers have reported that by being able to monitor student work during the week, by posting comments on the student home pages, or by annotating audio or video recordings, they are able to help students progress more quickly. These teachers have reported that iSCORE students progress more quickly than their peers, and remain keenly motivated to practise.

And so ... delve in!

The following pages will introduce you to the features of iSCORE. We begin with some quick and simple reference guides to get you started. The detailed user guide highlights all of the features of iSCORE and the underlying self-regulated learning cycle (planning, doing, and reflecting). This book also contains student exemplars that you can use to model the teaching and learning process. In addition, we regularly post new material on our website: www.iscorenews.com. Visit us online—and as the expression goes, "Like us on Facebook, follow us on Twitter"!

We are always looking for new ideas for using iSCORE. If you are willing to share some innovative or effective ways in which you or your students use iSCORE, please let us know by emailing us at info@iscorenews.com.

References

Abrami, P. C., & Barrett, H. (2005). Directions for research and development on electronic portfolios. *Canadian Journal of Learning and Technology, 31*(3), 1–15.

Abrami, P.C., Venkatesh, V., Meyer, E., & Wade, A. (in press). Using electronic portfolios to foster literacy and self-regulated learning skills in elementary students. *Journal of Educational Psychology*.

Barry, N. H., & Hallam, S. (2002). Practice. In R. Parncutt & G. E. McPherson (Eds.), *The science and psychology of music performance: Creative strategies for teaching and learning* (pp. 151–166). New York: Oxford University Press.

Bartolome, S. J. (2009). Naturally emerging self-regulated practice behaviors among highly successful beginning recorder students. *Research Studies in Music Education, 31*(1), 37–51.

Brook, J., Troop, M., & Upitis, R. (2011). Developing Self-Regulatory Skills in Learning to Play an Instrument. *Paper Presented at the Seventh International Research in Music Education Conference.* University of Exeter, Exeter, UK.

Centre for the Study of Learning and Performance, Queen's University, & The Royal Conservatory. (2012, January). iSCORE. Montreal, QC: Centre for the Study of Learning and Performance, Concordia University. Version 1.0. Location: http://grover.concordia.ca/iscore/2012

Dignath, C., Buettner, G., & Langfeldt, H-P. (2008). How can primary school students learn self-regulated learning strategies most effectively? A meta-analysis on self-regulation training programmes. *Educational Research Review, 3,* 101–129.

Feldman, S. (2010). *RCM: A quantitative investigation of teachers associated with the RCM exam process.* Toronto, ON: Susan Feldman & Associates.

Hallam, S. (1995). Professional musicians' orientations to practice: Implications for teaching. *British Journal of Music Education, 12*(1), 3–19.

Hallam, S. (2012). What predicts long-term commitment to actively engage with music? *Paper presented at the 24th Seminar on Research in Music Education, International Society for Music Education (ISME),* Thessaloniki, Greece.

Hallam, S., & Bautista, A. (2012). Processes of instrumental learning: The development of musical expertise. In G. McPherson & G. Welsh (Eds.), *The Oxford handbook of music education (Vol. 1).* (pp. 658–676). Oxford: Oxford University Press.

Kennell, R. (2002). Systematic research in studio instruction. In R. Colwell & C. Richardson (Eds.), *The handbook of research in music teaching and learning* (pp. 243–256). New York, NY: Oxford University Press.

McPherson, G. E., Davidson, J. W., & Faulkner, R. (2012). *Music in our lives: Redefining musical development, ability and identity.* Oxford: Oxford University Press.

McPherson, G.E., & Renwick, J. M. (2001). A longitudinal study of self-regulation in children's musical practice. *Music Education Research, 3*(2), 169–186.

McPherson, G. E., & Renwick, J. M. (2011). Self-regulation and mastery of musical skills. In B. J. Zimmerman & D. H. Schunk (Eds.), *Handbook of self-regulation of learning and performance* (pp. 234–248). New York: Routledge.

McPherson, G. E., & Zimmerman, B. J. (2011). Self-regulation of musical learning: A social cognitive perspective on developing performance skills. In R. Colwell & P. Webster (Eds.), *MENC handbook of research on music learning. Volume 2: Applications* (pp. 130–175). New York: Oxford University Press.

Miksza, P. (2007). Effective practice: An investigation of observed practice behaviors, self-reported practice habits, and the performance achievement of high school wind players. *Journal of Research in Music Education, 55*, 359–375. doi: 10.1177/0022429408317513

Sameroff, A. (2010). A unified theory of development: A dialectic integration of nature and nurture. *Child Development, 81*(1), 6–22.

Upitis, R., Abrami, P. C., Brook, J., Troop, M., & Catalano, L. (2010). Using ePEARL for music teaching: A case study. In G. Pérez-Bustamante, K. Physavat, & F. Ferreria (Eds.), *Proceedings of the International Association for Scientific Knowledge Conference* (pp. 36–45). Seville, Spain: IASK Press.

Zellers, M., & Mudrey, R. R. (2007). Electronic portfolios and metacognition: A phenomenological examination of the implementation of e-portfolios from the instructors' perspective. *International Journal of Instructional Media, 34*, 419–430.

Zhukov, K. (2009). Effective practising: A research perspective. *Australian Journal of Music Education, 1,* 3–12.

Zimmerman, B. J., & Schunk, D. H. (2011). Self-regulated learning and performance: An introduction and overview. In B. J. Zimmerman & D. H. Schunk (Eds.), *Handbook of self-regulation and performance* (pp. 1–12). New York: Routledge.

QUICK REFERENCE GUIDES [1]

---

[1] All of these quick reference guides can be downloaded as pdf files from our website: www.iscorenews.com

Choosing Your Settings

Begin customizing your iSCORE profile by choosing your settings:

1. Log into your account at www.rcmusic.ca.
2. Click on Settings in the upper right-hand corner.
3. Customize your settings.
4. Click Save after you have chosen your settings.

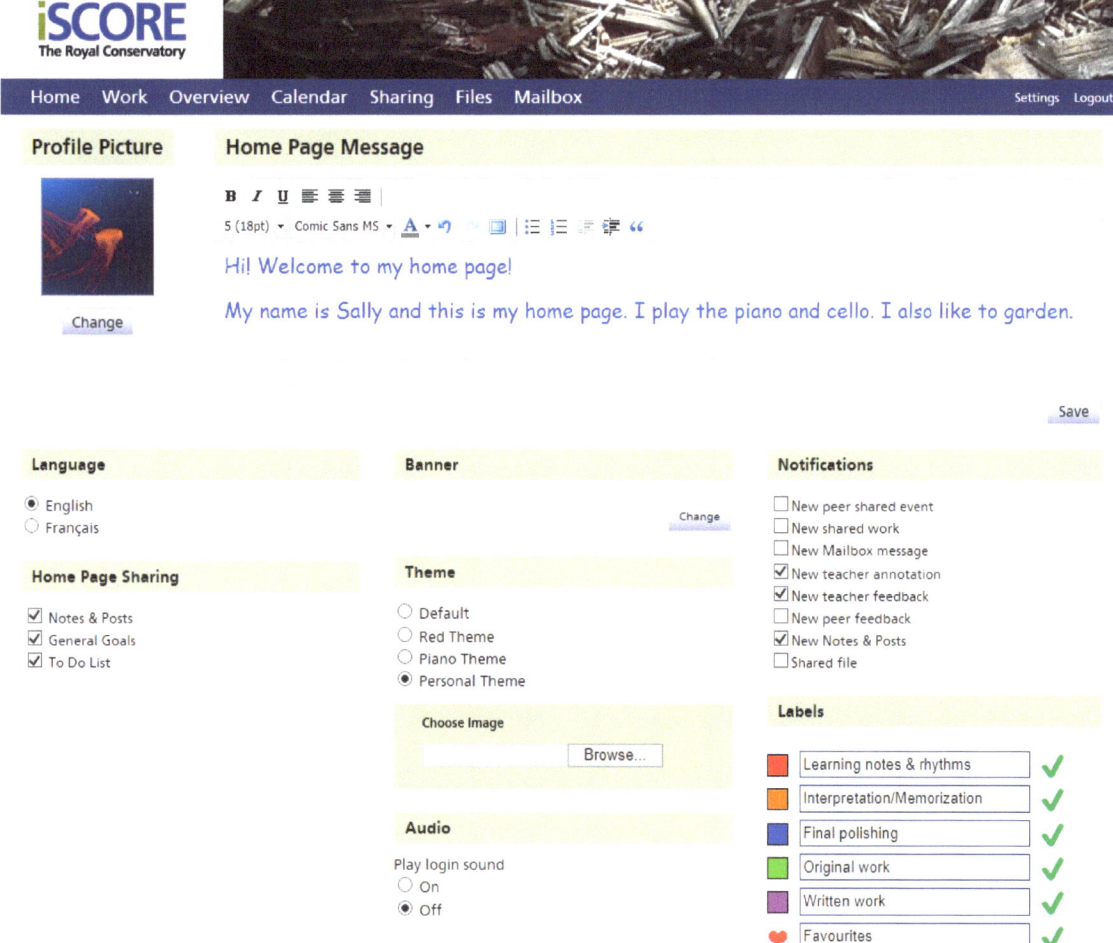

To add your own personal touch to your portfolio:

1. Click on Change to choose the background banner for your home page from the iSCORE banner bank, or from your own image collection.
2. Click on Change to choose the profile picture for your home page from the iSCORE image bank, or from your own image collection.
3. Write your own message on the home page.
4. Choose your layout theme.
5. Choose your preferred language (English or French).
6. Activate/deactivate the welcome chime (Audio).
7. Select the parts of your home page you would like to share.

To customize your settings even further:

1. Choose the iSCORE activities about which you would like to be notified.
2. Set colour codes for labelling your work projects instead of using the default labels.

Notes & Posts

The Notes & Posts function is one great way to facilitate communication in your studio through iSCORE. You will find it in the lower left corner of any student or teacher home page. To see how this feature links directly to teaching, see the iSCORE iDEA called *Using iSCORE to Practise* (p. 93).

You can leave a note on your own home page. To leave a note for someone else, you have to go to that person's home page. (See p. 23 to learn how to navigate to another person's home page.)

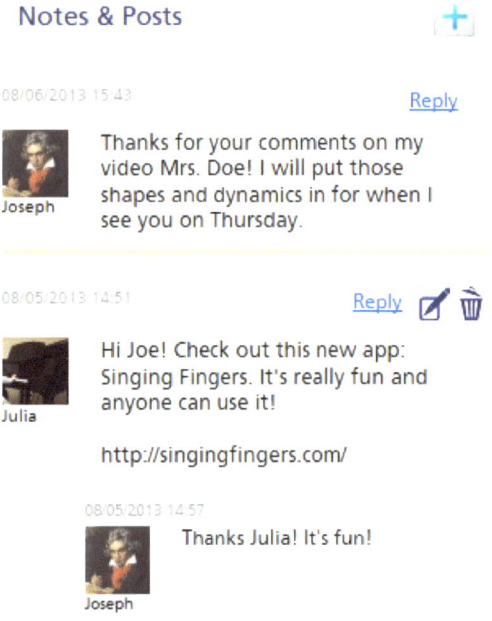

To write a new message on *your* Notes & Posts:

1. Click on ![+]
2. Write your post.
3. Attach a file by clicking "Attach File" and choosing a file from your iSCORE filing cabinet, which will be displayed in a pop-up window.
4. If you want to add a URL, copy the address directly into the text box. Note that this URL is not a live link. If you want to attach a live link, first create a link under your Files tab, and then the link will be live in Notes & Posts.
5. Click on the green checkmark ✓ to save the post or on the ✗ to cancel the post.
6. To view older posts, click on `<< Older`
7. To move back to viewing more recent posts, click on `Newer >>`

To Share your Notes & Posts with others:

1. Go to *Sharing*.

2. Click on ➕ Share to select the class, and then select the whole class or one or more students.

3. To unshare, click on Unshare

Trouble-shooting tip: Make sure your Notes & Posts are checked off in the Home Page Sharing section of the Settings page.

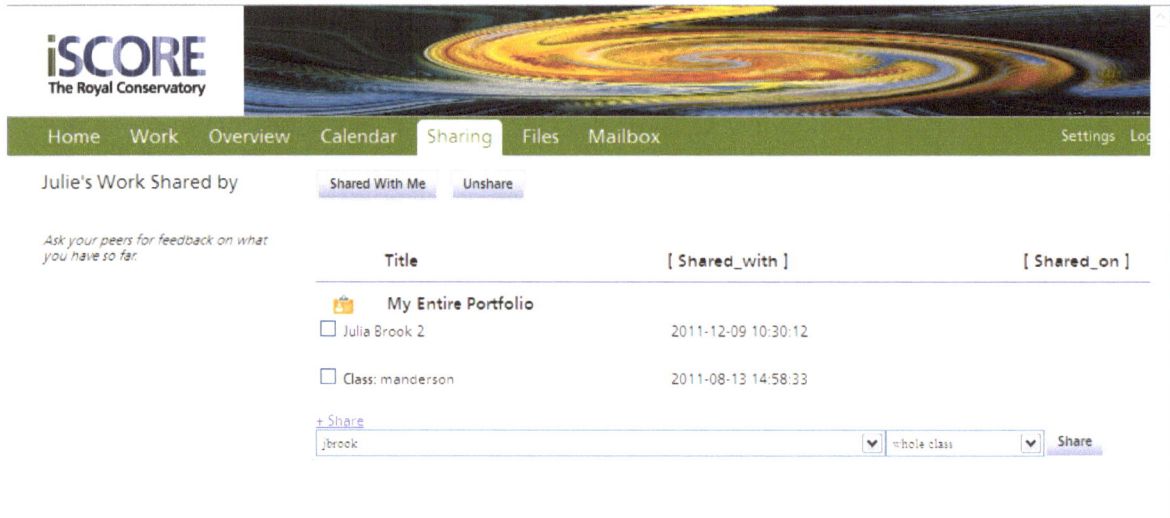

To Get to Another Home Page

Students need to:

1. Click on Sharing in the upper home page menu.
2. Click on Shared With Me
3. Click on the 👁 icon next to the name of the peer.

4. Write a post using the same steps for writing a post on your own portfolio.

Teachers can also access home pages of their students or linked colleagues through their iSCORE manage page:

1. Click on iSCORE Manage.
2. Click on My Students.
3. Click on the symbol next to the name of the student.
4. Write a post using the same steps for writing a post on your own portfolio.

Leaving a Post on Someone's Home Page

1. Click the + icon in the upper right corner of the Notes & Posts box.
2. Type a message in the box that opens up.
3. Click on ✔ above the text box, once you have finished typing in your message.

Other Important Notes & Posts Features

To cancel a post:

1. Click on

To add an attachment to a post:

1. Click on Attach File above the text box and it will open up your iSCORE file cabinet.
2. Select your desired file and click Add to add the attachment to your post.

To reply to a post:

1. Click on Reply (located on the upper right of a post).
2. Your reply will appear as an indented response to the original post.

Finding and Pasting Links

There are many Internet resources that you might want to link to your work in iSCORE. Many teachers link to videos from YouTube. To see how this feature can be used in practice, see *Using iSCORE to Compare Performances* in the iSCORE iDEAS section of this guide (p. 89).

To find a link, search the www.youtube.com site. Once you've located the video, copy the URL that appears in the top left bar of the screen.

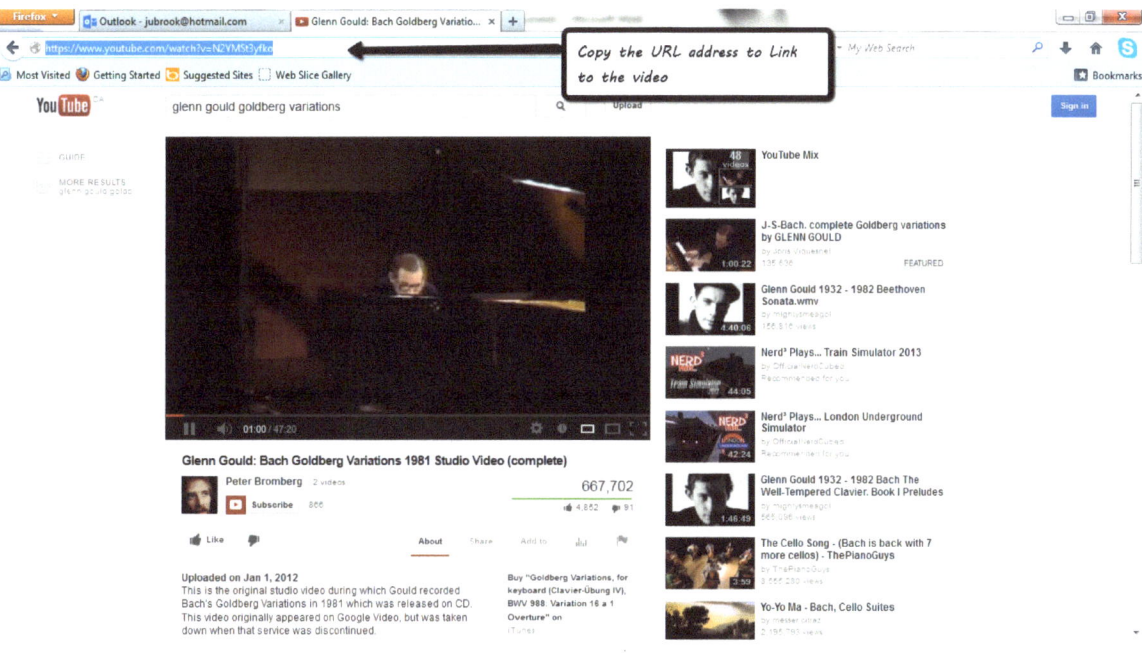

Open a previous "Work" project or create a new one by clicking on the work tab and then clicking "Add."

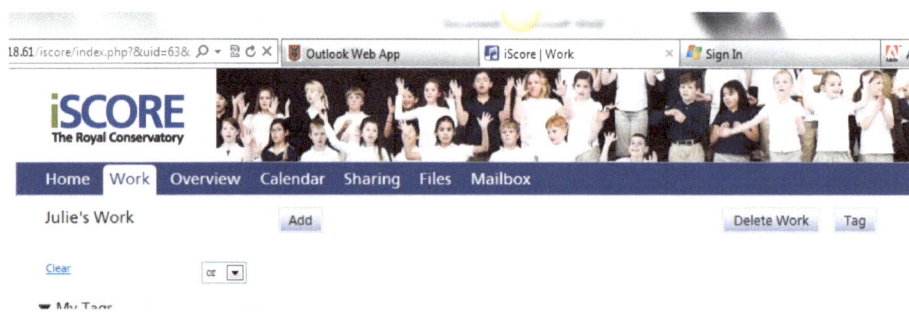

Click "Doing." Then click the link icon (🔗) and paste your link to the YouTube video in the field under the word "Link." You're done!

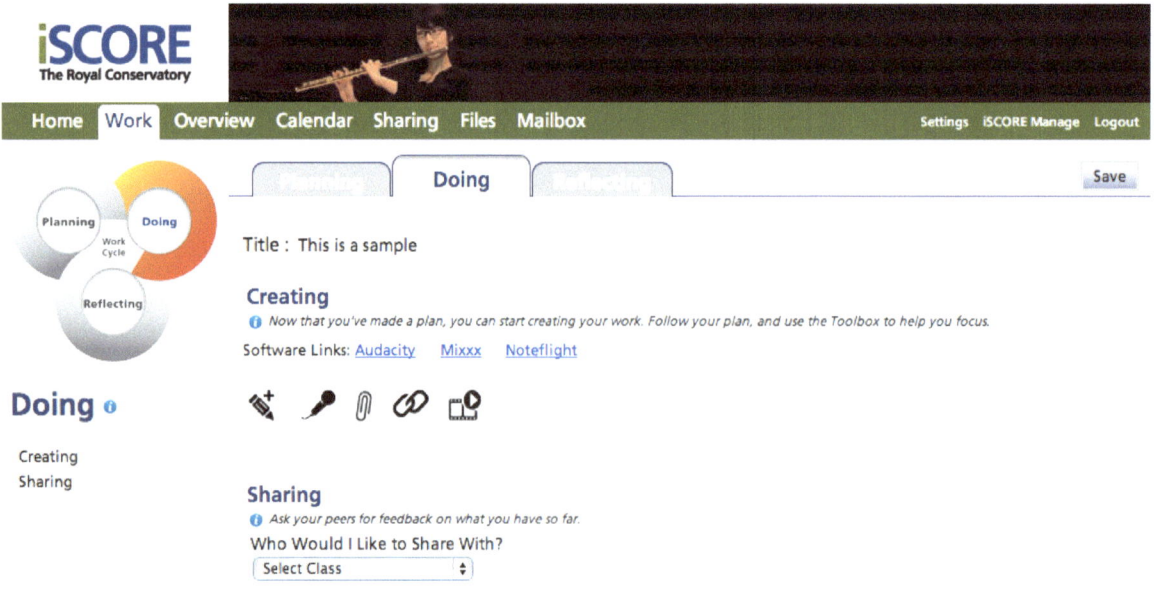

Using the Annotator

You can annotate your student's video/audio recording that has been uploaded in the iSCORE media tool. This is a great way for teachers to give feedback to students between lessons. You can make either a text annotation or a recorded annotation. To see how this tool can be used in practice, see *Using iSCORE to Help with Ear Training* (p. 100), and the Student Exemplars (e.g., *Using iSCORE for a Quick Study: Bagatelle* (p. 122).

Uploading Media into Your *Teacher* Portfolio

1. Click on Work on the horizontal menu.
2. Click on a specific piece of work or work title.
3. Click on the Media icon
4. Click on "Click to Upload Media".
5. Upload audio/video files from your computer.

Trouble-shooting tip: Sometimes videos need to be compressed before they can be uploaded successfully. For example, an AVI video could take hours to upload! Experiment with different video converters to see what works best on your system. Some students have had good experiences with Miro Video Converter (www.mirovideoconverter.com). It's free.

Trouble-shooting tip: Your media file format is compatible with iSCORE if it is one of the following:

avi	Audio Video Interleave File	mp4	MPEG-4 Video File
flv	Flash Video File	ogg	Ogg
mpeg	MPEG-1 System format	rm	Real Media File
m4a	MPEG-4 Audio File	wav	WAVE Audio File
m4v	MPEG-4 Video format	wma	Windows Media Audio File
mov	Apple QuickTime Movie	wmv	Windows Media Video File
mp3	MPEG audio layer 3		

Uploading Media into Your *Student's* Portfolio

1. Access your student's portfolio through iSCORE Manage.
2. Click on Work on the horizontal menu.
3. Click on Doing.
4. Scroll to the bottom of the Doing page and click on Add Media.
5. Click on Upload new media.
6. Upload audio/video files from your computer.

Adding an Annotation to a Video/Audio Recording

1. Access your student's portfolio through iSCORE Manage.
2. Click on Work on the horizontal menu.
3. Select the title of the work you want to annotate.
4. Click on the Doing tab to access the recording.
5. Play the video/audio recording and pause it where you want to add an annotation.
6. Click on either ⊕T to make a text annotation, or 🎤 to record your annotation.

Adding a Text Annotation

1. Click on ⊕
2. Type in the annotation text.
3. Choose how long you want the annotation to be displayed for while the video is playing. The timing is important so that your intent is clear for the student.
4. Click on Save.

Adding a Recorded Annotation

1. Click on 🎤
2. A red microphone icon will show up on the right side of the video.
3. Click on the red microphone icon to start the recording.
4. When you click on the red microphone icon, you will first see an Adobe Flash Player Settings window pop up, asking to access the computer's camera and microphone. In order for this feature to work, you must click on Allow.
5. The recording will start immediately.
6. When you are finished with your recording, click on the red stop button.
7. Remember to click on Save before leaving the page.

When playing a video or audio recording, the audio annotations pause the recording, whereas the text annotations are displayed while the recording continues to play.

Using The Calendar

Use the calendar to schedule rehearsals, lessons, or concerts.

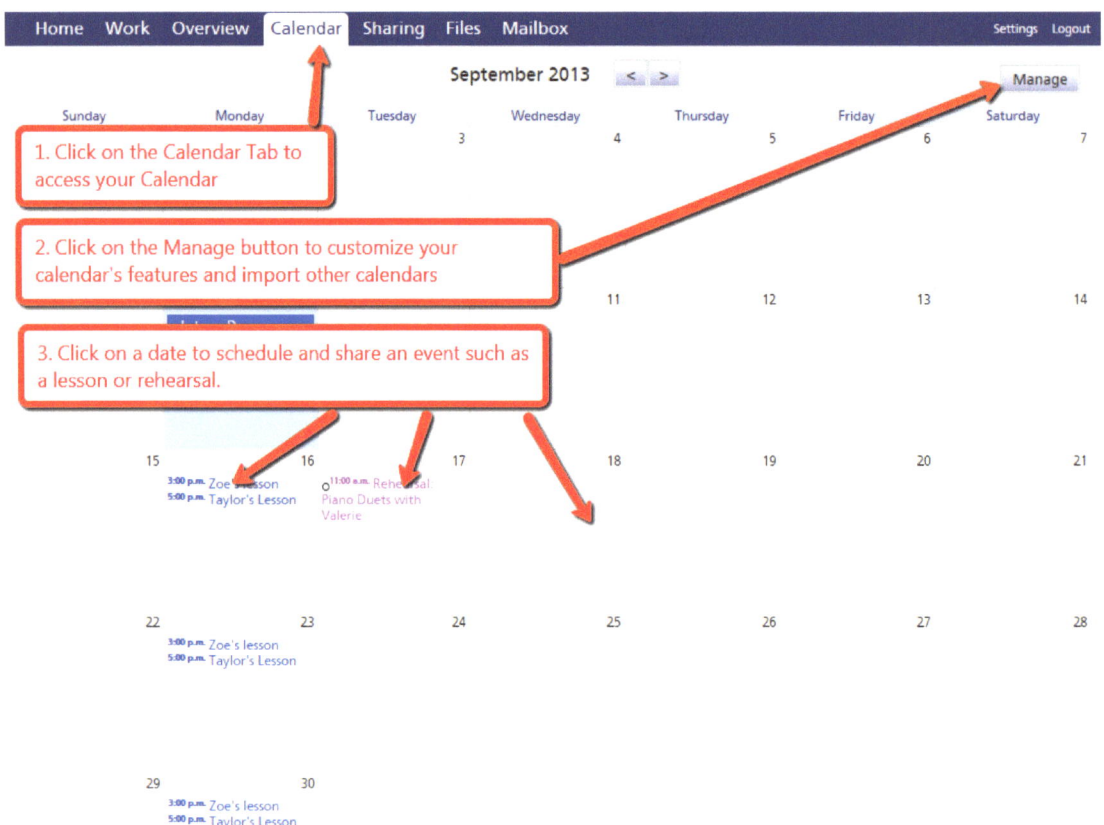

Creating Categories in Your Calendar

The **Manage My Calendar** section is where you can create different colour-coded categories to organize your events such as lessons, recitals, rehearsals, competitions, or exams.

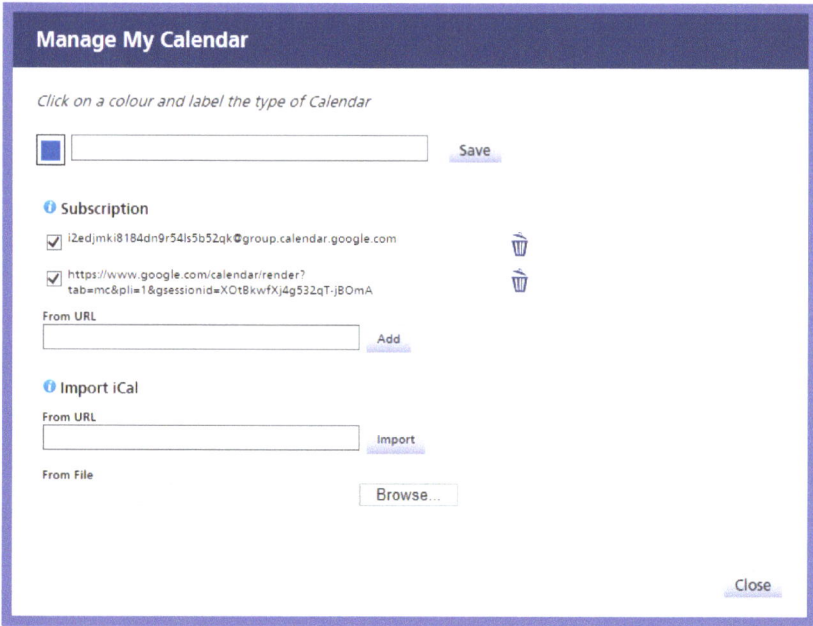

1. Access Manage My Calendar by clicking on the Manage button in the upper right-hand corner of the Calendar.

2. Click on the coloured square on the left side to bring up the column of colours to choose from.

3. Type the category name in the blank beside it and click Save.

4. Repeat as often as you would like and remember to save your choices; you are always free to change your choices later.

The Calendar is versatile; it can adapt to existing calendar applications.

1. If you subscribe to an online calendar, type the URL in the Subscription field and then click Add.

2. If you want to upload your iCal file from your computer, click on Browse to upload the filename or click on Import to provide the URL if you store it online. Note that your iCal needs to have been exported to a place like the desktop before browsing and uploading.

Creating and Sharing Events in Your Calendar

Now that your event categories have been set, you can start to create and share events. When you create an event in your calendar, such as a lesson time slot or a recital, you can share this schedule with your whole studio or just selected students. This way, students or fellow teachers in your studio can see any lesson schedules, changes, or other events. The calendar events will appear on the home page under Upcoming Events.

Quick Reference Guides 33

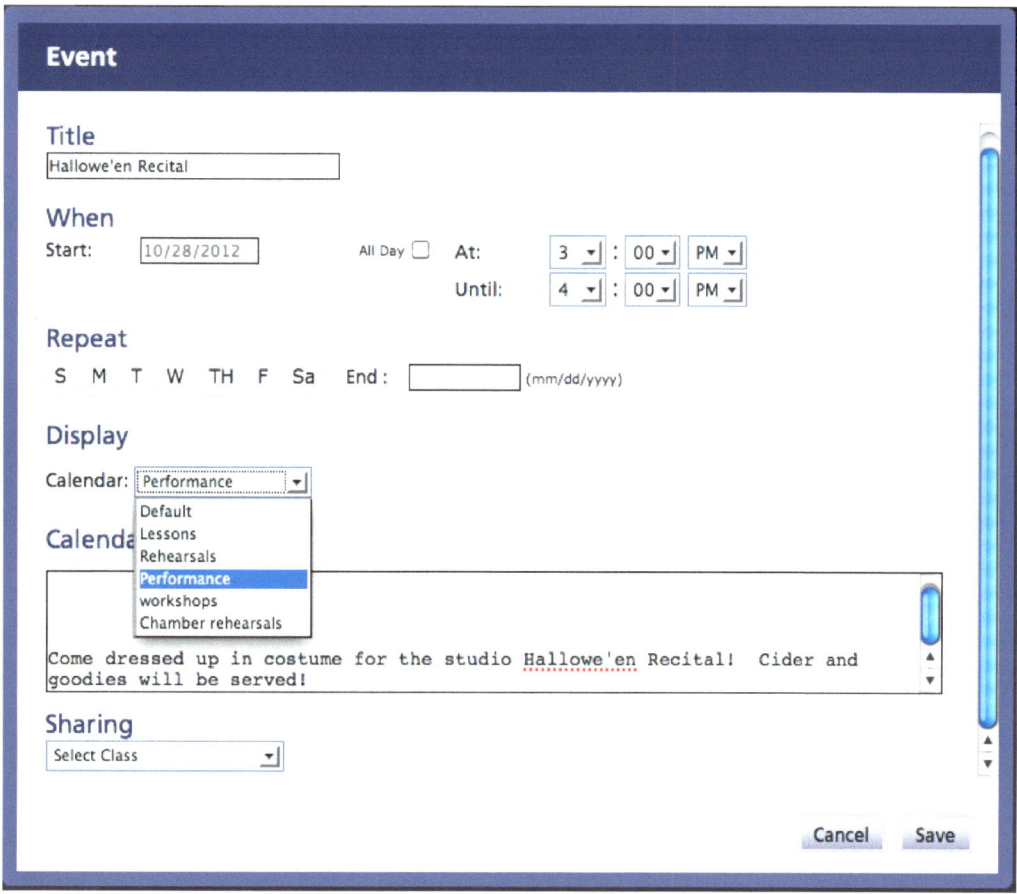

1. Click on any date on the Calendar where you want to schedule an event.
2. An Event page will pop up and you can enter the title of your event.
3. Uncheck the All Day box to specify a start and end time for your event.
4. Click on the day(s) you want this event to repeat (such as lesson times) and type in an End date if needed.
5. Click on the drop-down menu under Display to choose a category for this event. The colour you chose for the category in the Manage section will be the colour in which your event appears in the Calendar.
6. Type an event description in the Calendar Description box.
7. Click on the drop-down menu under Sharing to choose those with whom you want to share this event.
8. Remember to click on Save when you are finished!

Using iSCORE Files

Your iSCORE portfolio contains an online file cabinet, where you can collect resources to share with students and/or teaching colleagues.

Uploading Resources to Your Files Tab

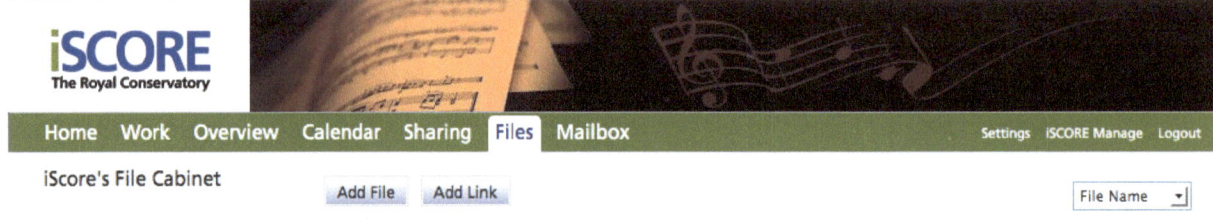

To access your iSCORE file cabinet, click on the Files tab on the horizontal menu.

1. Click on Add File to upload any file, such as a pdf, MS Word document, or MP3.
2. Click on Add Link to enter in the URL address of a website.

Your iSCORE file cabinet is preloaded with many resources in both French and English. These include:

1. Lesson plans.
2. Articles on self-regulated learning (handy to send to parents!).
3. Videos about iSCORE.

Viewing and Sorting Your Files

The items in the filing cabinet can be sorted for easier viewing by using the sidebar on the left.

My Files: Shows the files you have uploaded.

All Files: Shows all the files in the filing cabinet.

Files Shared With Me: Shows files shared with you.

Resources: Files developed by the iSCORE team for support.

Links: All the links in the filing cabinet.

Your files can be filtered by File type or Resource type. Click the box beside the desired type.

To Add a File

1. Click Add File.
2. Click on Browse to choose a file.
3. Add your file.
4. Click Save to upload it.

To Add a Link

1. Click Add Link.
2. Type in a Title for your link and paste the URL.
3. Click Save.

Sharing Your Files

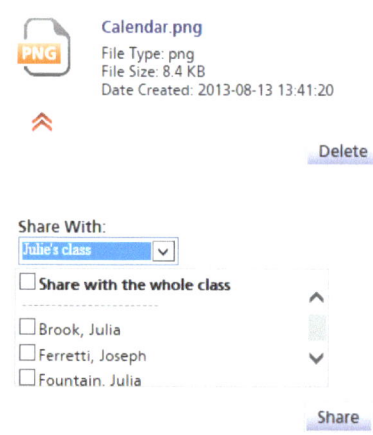

Storing resources in your iSCORE Files allows you to store and share resources easily with your students and colleagues.

From Files tab to Files tab: To share a link or a file, allowing it to appear in another person's File tab, do the following:

1. Click on the file icon to open up the sharing feature.
2. Select the class and member of the class with whom you want to share the file in the pop-up drop-down menu and click on Share.
3. You may also share an item with the whole class.
4. These files will now appear in the person's Files tab.

Attaching Files with Notes & Posts or the Mailbox: Items in your iSCORE Files can be attached in the Notes & Posts area on your home page. They can also be attached with messages in the iSCORE Mailbox. These features allow you to send and receive resources without having to clutter your own personal mail browser. Follow these steps:

1. Click on Attach File.
2. Select the file you want to share.
3. Click on Add.

DETAILED USER GUIDE

iSCORE Manage

iSCORE Manage is where you create new classes, invite your students to join your iSCORE classes, and view your students' iSCORE portfolios. Students must create their RCM accounts before they can accept invitations. This process is described in the e-mail instructions sent in the invitation from the RCM.

Students are organized into classes and you create these classes in iSCORE Manage.

To access iSCORE Manage, Click on **iSCORE Manage** (at the top right of your iSCORE Home page).

What is a class?

A class is a group of students' portfolios. All your students need to be in a group or a class. You can keep all your students in one class or you can separate them into various groups according to your different needs. It is possible to have students in more than one class.

My Classes

This is the section where you create a new class and where you can view your students' portfolios.

Creating a New Class:

1. Click on "My Classes," which is located on the sidebar.
2. To create a new class, enter the name of your class in the text box at the bottom of the screen.
3. This new class will be added to your list of classes.
4. Once this class is created you can click "Invite Students" to send invitations to students to join.
5. You can change the name of your class by clicking on "Edit Name".
6. You can view the students' portfolios in this class by clicking "View Students".

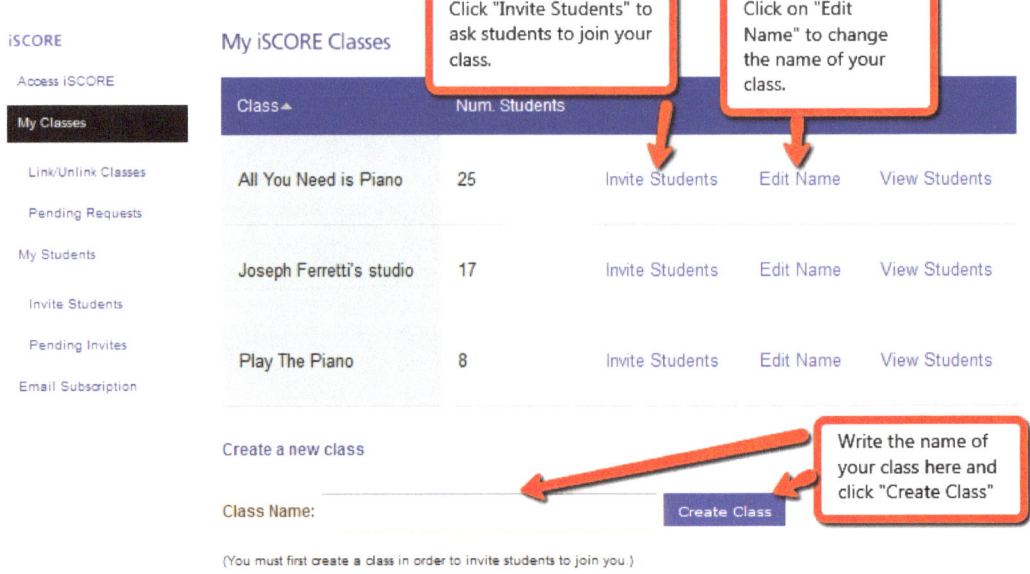

Inviting Students to Join a Class:

1. Click on "Invite Students" on the sidebar.
2. Select the class that you want your students to join, from the drop-down menu.
3. Enter the student's e-mail address in the box.
4. Invite multiple students at one time by separating each e-mail address with a comma.
5. Students *with* iSCORE accounts will receive an e-mail asking them to join the class.
6. Students *without* iSCORE accounts will receive an e-mail asking them to create an iSCORE account.

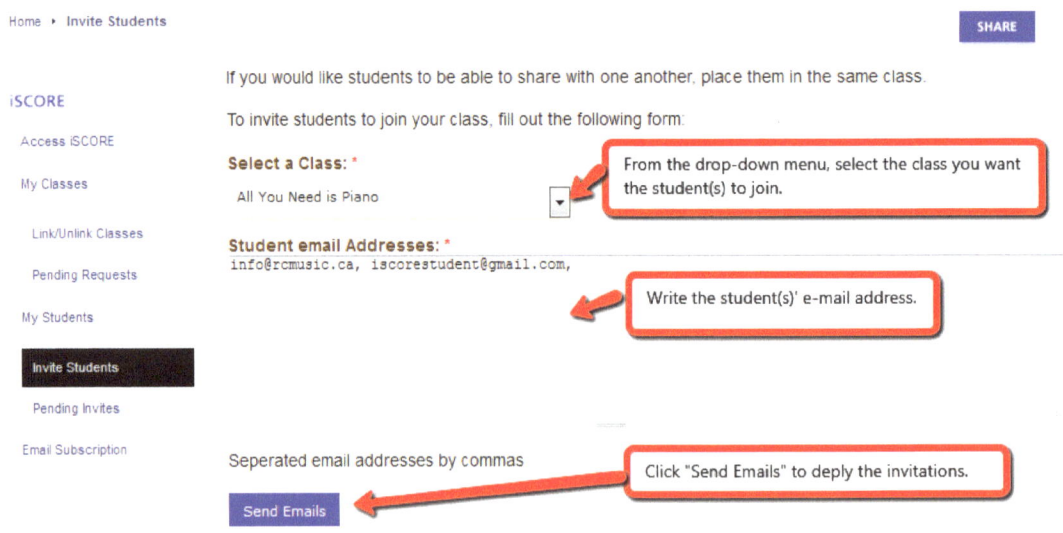

Pending Invites: You can see if a student has accepted your request to join a class.

1. Click on "Pending Invites" on the sidebar to view invitations you have sent.
2. Click on "Resend invite" to send your invitation again.
3. Click on "Cancel invite" to withdraw your invitation.
4. You will also be notified by e-mail when your student accepts your invitation.

Link/Unlink Classes

The Link/unlink tab allows you to connect or disconnect from a class. Unlinking from a class does NOT delete students' iSCORE accounts or dismantle the class. Click Link/Unlink in the last column of the desired class.

Status	Class Code	Class	
Linked	1015	Debbie's studio	Unlink
Linked	1489	Tuesday Evenings Jam	Unlink
Linked	1510	Theory Class	Unlink
Unlinked	1512	New Class	Link

Pending Requests

Pending requests is the section where you can see requests from students to join your class.

Click "Accept Request" to have the student join your iSCORE class.

Click "Reject Request" if you do not want this person to be part of your class.

Once you accept a request, the student's name will be removed from the Pending Requests section and appear under the My Students & My Classes sections.

My Students

This is the section where you can see all of your students. You can also filter your student list by class and view your students' iSCORE portfolios.

To filter by class: Select the class from the drop-down menu by "Filter by Class".

To View a student's iSCORE portfolio: Click on "View" in the iSCORE Portfolio column beside the student's name.

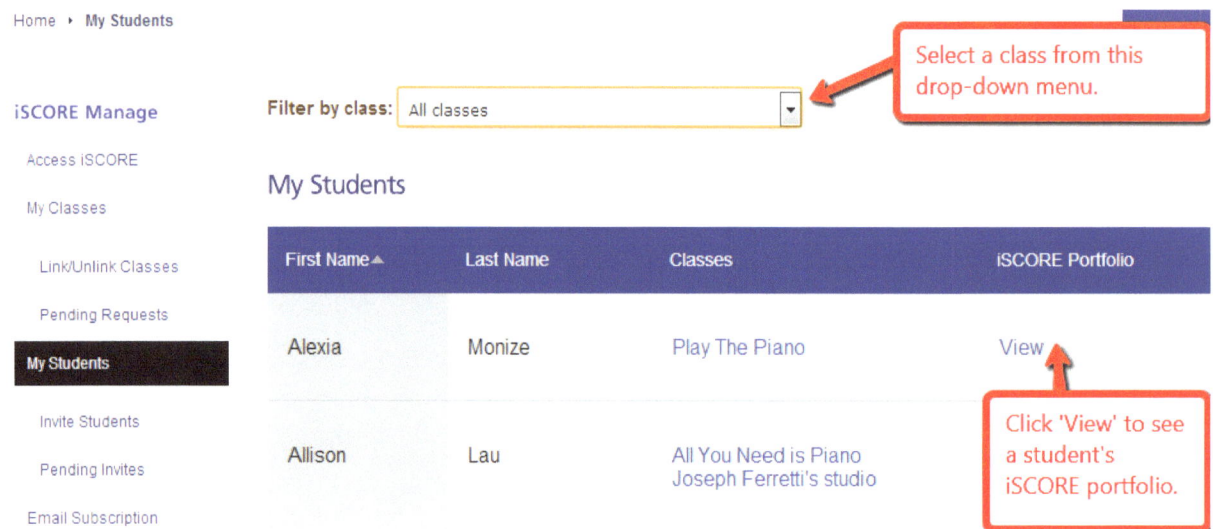

Invite Students

This is the place where you can invite students to your class.

To invite students to a class:
1. Select the class (See the "Create class section" to find out how to create a class).
2. Enter the e-mail address associated with your student.
3. Enter as many student invites as you like. Separate each e-mail address with a comma.
4. Click "Send e-mails".

5. Your students will receive an e-mail invitation with simple instructions on how to join the class. Once they accept your invitation by following the e-mail instructions they will be in your class and they will have an iSCORE portfolio.

Trouble-shooting tip: In order to be able to share with each other, students must be in the same class. Keep this in mind when creating your classes.

Students Requesting to Join Your Class

Students can request to join your class.
If the student does **NOT** have an RCM account, s/he can do this from the rcmusic.ca website from the Login button. Tell the student to click on "Sign Up for an RCM Account" on www.rcmusic.ca and follow these instructions (you might want to photocopy these instructions for your students):

1. Click on "Login" at the top right corner.
2. Select "Sign Up for an RCM Account" in that window.
3. Complete the form.
4. Click on "Submit" when you are done. (Remember to write down the password you chose!)
5. Close your browser.
6. You will receive an e-mail with a link to verify your account.
7. When you click on the link you will be taken to the My Account Page.
8. Continue with the instructions for someone with an RCM account (below).

If the student already has an RCM account, he or she can do this from the www.rcmusic.ca website under "My Account".

1. Select "I use iSCORE".
2. Select "I will use iSCORE as a Student".
3. Select your teacher from the drop-down menu.
4. Select the appropriate class from your teacher's class list.
5. Once you make these selections, an e-mail will be sent to your teacher asking them to include you in their iSCORE class. This request will also appear in "Pending Invites" in the iSCORE Manage section. Once the teacher accepts this request, the student will appear in the class.

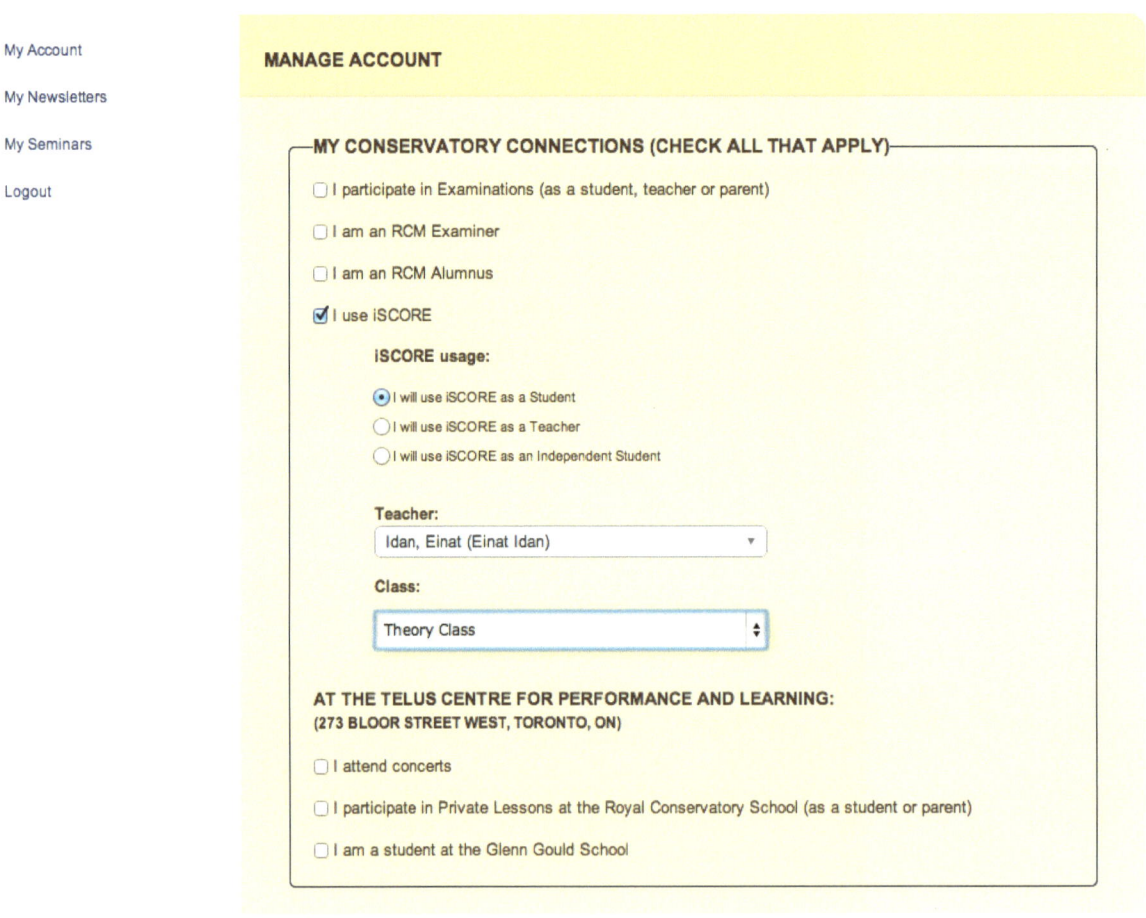

Teacher Tags

You can create tags (labels) that can be attached to your students' work so that you can organize the work that you have seen. Teacher Tags will appear on the sidebar when you are viewing a student's work. These Teacher Tags will not be visible to the students, so you can use them for your own purposes.

To assign a tag to your student's project:

1. Select your student's project(s) in the Work Index.
2. Click 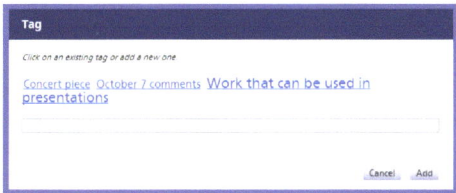 on to see your tags or add a new one.
3. Select a tag or add a new one.
4. This tag will now be associated with that project.

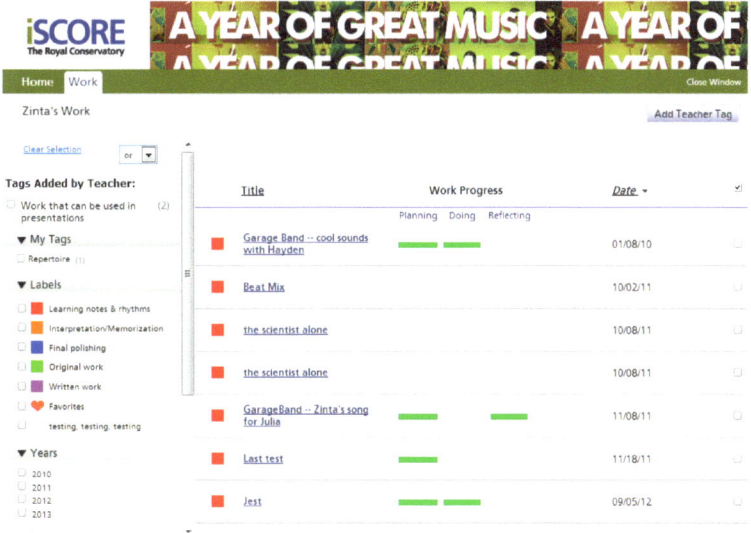

To see all the work that has a particular tag select a tag on the left-hand side and the associated projects will appear. Sample tags include: pieces that have annotations, work with new comments, priority, etc.

Home

This is the first page you see when you enter your portfolio. You can personalize your home page (change the look and feel of it) by using the settings page. The home page also displays your long-term general goals and items to complete in the shorter term, as listed in the To Do List. You can also communicate with others through the Notes & Posts. On the bottom of your home page, there is a bell that tells you if you have any new Notifications. Upcoming Events are also posted at the top.

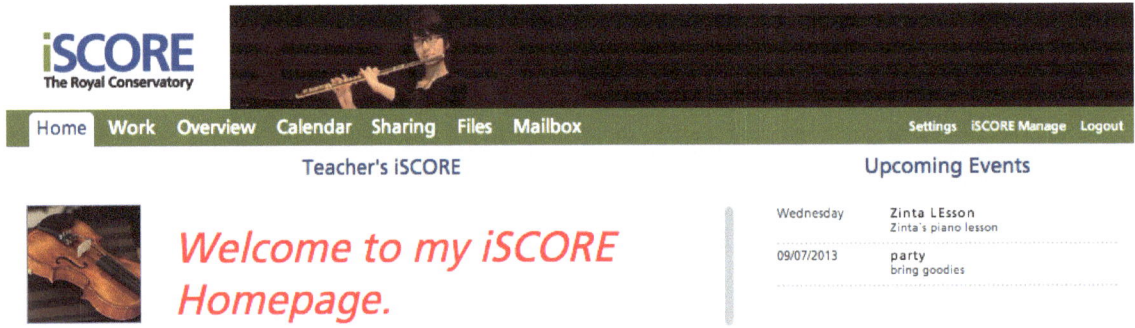

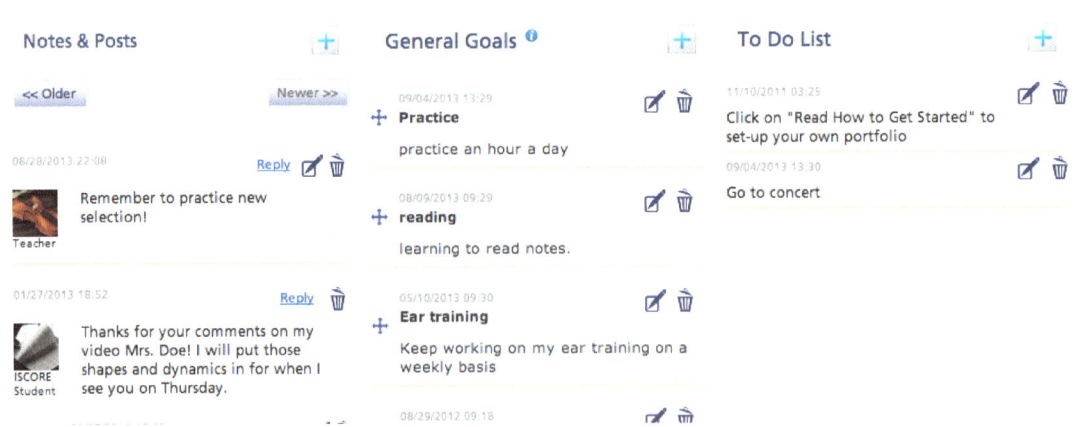

Settings

Begin customizing and personalizing your iSCORE portfolio by choosing your settings:

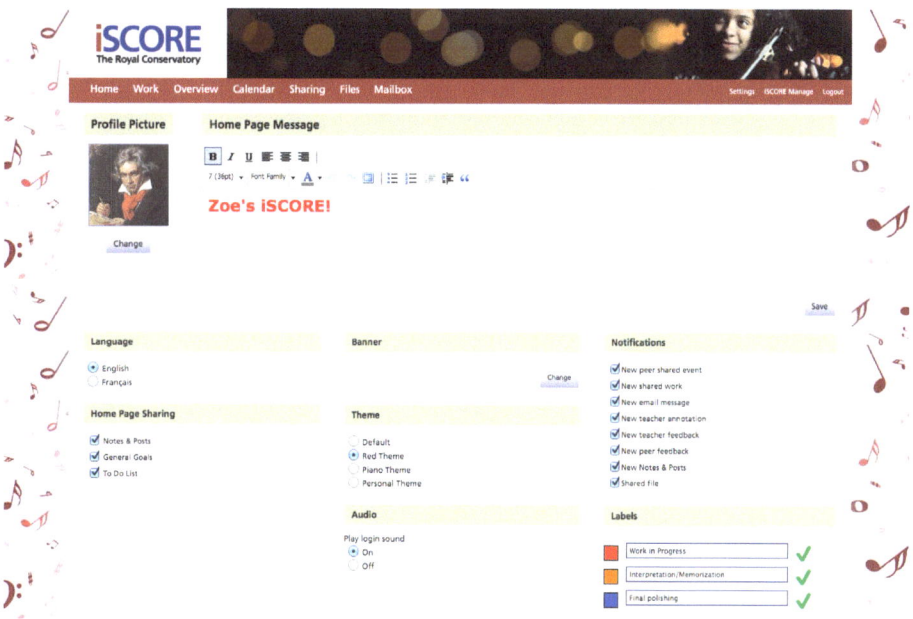

1. Click on Settings in the upper right-hand corner.
2. Choose the aspect of your home page that you would like to personalize or change.
3. To personalize your home page message, type your own words in the text editor. You can choose different types of fonts and colours.
4. Choose your profile picture from the iSCORE bank of images or from your own image collection.
5. Choose the background banner for your home page from the iSCORE banner bank or upload an image from your own collection that is 800 x 90 pixels in size.

6. Choose your layout theme from the iSCORE choices, or click "Personal Theme" to upload your own layout theme.
7. Choose your preferred language (English or French).
8. Activate/deactivate the welcome chime under the Audio setting.
9. To change a label, type in your own text and click on the green checkmark.
10. Select items that you would like to be notified about under notifications.
11. Select the items you would like to share with others under the Home Page Sharing bar.
12. Click Save after you choose your settings.
13. Click Home to return to your home page.

General Goals

General goals are long-term learning goals that you and your students can set (e.g., getting faster at learning pieces, beginning to compose pieces, or planning for a concert or exam). To write a general goal:

1. Click on ➕
2. Name the type of goal in the title box (e.g., exam).
3. Describe your goal in the box below the title box.

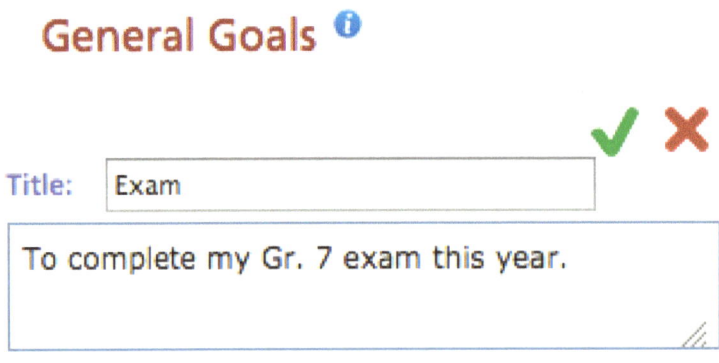

4. Click ✓ to save or on the ✗ to cancel the general goal.

5. Repeat Steps 1, 2, 3, & 4 for each new general goal.

To modify your general goal(s):

1. Click the pencil icon ✎ to edit a goal.
2. Change your text.
3. Click the green checkmark ✓ to save edited goal.
4. Click the trash can 🗑 to delete a goal entirely.
5. Drag the cross-arrows icon ✣ to rearrange the order of your goals.

To Do List

This is where you write the tasks that you'd like to complete over a relatively short period of time, say, a week or two.

To write item(s):

1. Click on ✚
2. Write your text.
3. Click on the green checkmark. ✓
4. Repeat steps 1, 2, & 3 for each additional item.

To edit an item:
1. Click on ✎
2. Edit text.
3. Click on the green checkmark ✓ to save the edited item.

To delete an item:

1. Click on 🗑

Notes & Posts

This is where you can send and receive messages from other iSCORE users. To write a new message on *your* Notes & Posts:

1. Click on ➕
2. Write your post.
3. Attach a file by clicking Attach File, and choosing a file from your iSCORE filing cabinet, which will be displayed in a pop-up window.
4. If you want to add a URL, copy the address directly into the text box. Note that this URL is not a live link. If you want to attach a live link, first create a link in your Files tab. Then the link will be live when you attach it to Notes & Posts.
5. Click on the green checkmark ✓ to save the post or on the ✗ to cancel the post.

To Share your Notes & Posts with others:

1. Go to *Sharing*.

2. Click on ➕ Share to select the class, and then select the whole class or one or more students.
3. To unshare, click on Unshare

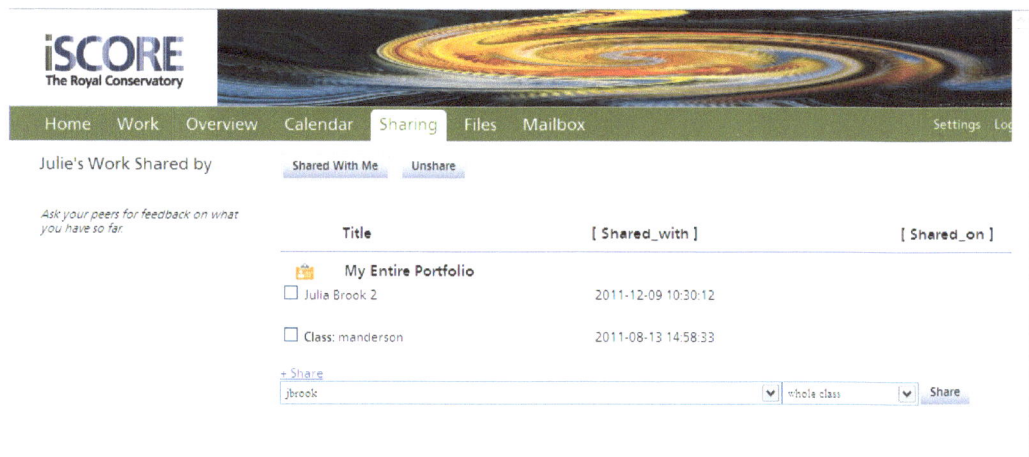

Note: Teachers have access to all their students' portfolios by default, via the iSCORE Manage section. However, students and teachers wishing to share with other teachers will have to share as described above.

To Write on Someone Else's Notes & Posts

1. Go to Sharing.
2. Click on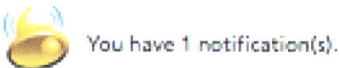
3. A list of all the people who have permitted you to view their portfolios will appear.
4. Click on the eye symbol beside the desired person.
5. This will take you to that person's home page.
6. Then write a message following the directions for posting on your own Notes & Posts.

Notifications

This is where you'll see that you have new messages and posts.

You have 1 notification(s).

Click on the bell to view and hide the notification details.

Upcoming Events

Refer to the Calendar section to learn how to add/edit Upcoming Events.

Work

This is where you plan, create, and reflect on your work. Your work can be anything from learning new repertoire, to improving aspects of your technique, to your creative stages in composing or improvising. Your work index shows the date, title, and progress (planning, doing, reflecting) of your work. You can also filter your work by clicking on the labels or tags in the sidebar. You can add new work as well as delete work. You can also add new tags and export your work.

1. To add new work, click on **Add**
2. To edit your work, click on the title of your work from the work index.
3. To select all of your work, click ✓
4. To export work, select the work you want to export and then click on **Export**
5. To import work, click on **Import** and browse and upload the chosen file.
6. To delete work, select the work to delete and click on **Delete Work**

Once you have started a new work, you will have access to three tabs: Planning, Doing and Reflecting. Each of these tabs will have items that you may complete or decide to skip, depending on your needs.

Planning

This is where you will plan your work. Click on the Planning tab.

Labels

Labels are colour codes that help you to organize your work by identifying various learning stages.

Use the default labels or create your own labels in Settings.

Task Description

A task description explains what you must do for a particular assignment or activity.

1. Click on ✏️ to open the text editor for the task description.
2. Type in your description. If you need help deciding what to write, click the ⓘ
3. Save your description by clicking ✓
4. To edit your task description, scroll your cursor over the text area and click on the pencil icon ✏️ and alter your text.
5. Click ✓ after making your edits.
6. To delete a task description, click on 🗑

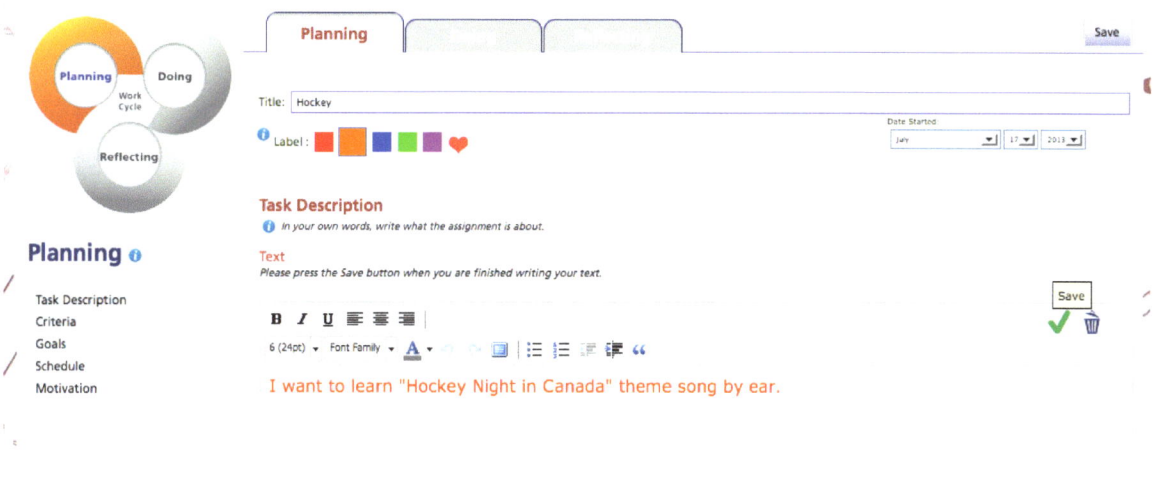

Criteria

Criteria describe the standards by which the work will be evaluated.

1. Click on ✏️ to type in the text editor.
2. Click on 📎 to attach a document or file.

3. Save your description by clicking ✓

4. Click to ✏️ edit your criteria.

5. Click ✓ after making your edits.

6. To delete your text, click 🗑️

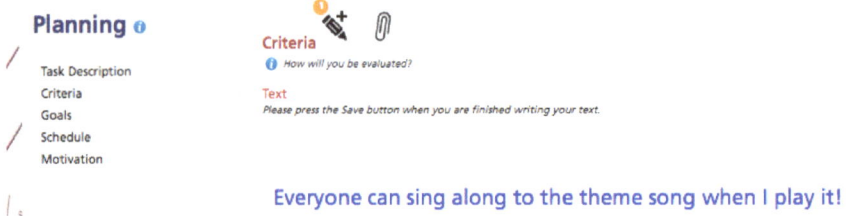

Goals

These goals relate to specific tasks (in contrast to the general goals on the home page). You can write or audio-record your goals (see steps 1 and 2 below) and also attach links and files that relate to your goals (see steps 3 and 4).). Large goals can be broken down into smaller supporting goals (see step 5) and strategies can also be identified.

1. Click on 🏁 to write your goal using the text editor.

2. Click on 🎤 to audio-record your goal.

3. Click on 📎 to attach a file to your goal.

4. Click on 🔗 to create a link to your goal.

5. Click on 📊 to open boxes to write supporting goals, or to break down your goal into smaller goals.

Strategies

Strategies are specific behaviours that will help you to achieve your task goals. You can document strategies that will help you achieve your goals.

1. Click on ![share icon] in the Goal section of the Planning Page.
2. Write the name of your strategy and click ✓ to save your strategy.

You can also click on the ![bank icon] to bring up the Strategy Bank that is located at the bottom of the screen and contains a list of all the strategies you have documented in your portfolio. Select a strategy by clicking on the checkbox next to it to add it to your plan. Once you select a strategy, it will be saved to your plan.

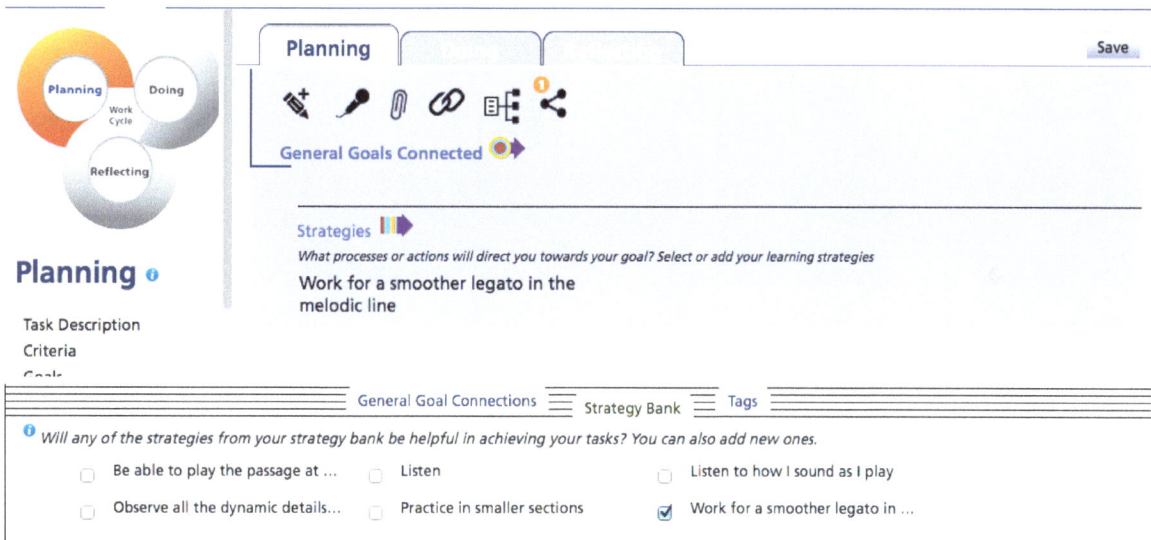

General Goal Connections

Click on the ⦿▸ in the Task Goal section to bring up the General Goal Connections tab from the bottom of the screen: you can link any general goals that are relevant to this task goal. Once you select a general goal by clicking on the checkbox next to it, it will be saved to your plan. As you connect your projects to specific general goals, the Overview section will display each general goal and show how many works are linked to it. That way, you will be able to review, which general goals are being addressed, and which ones are being neglected.

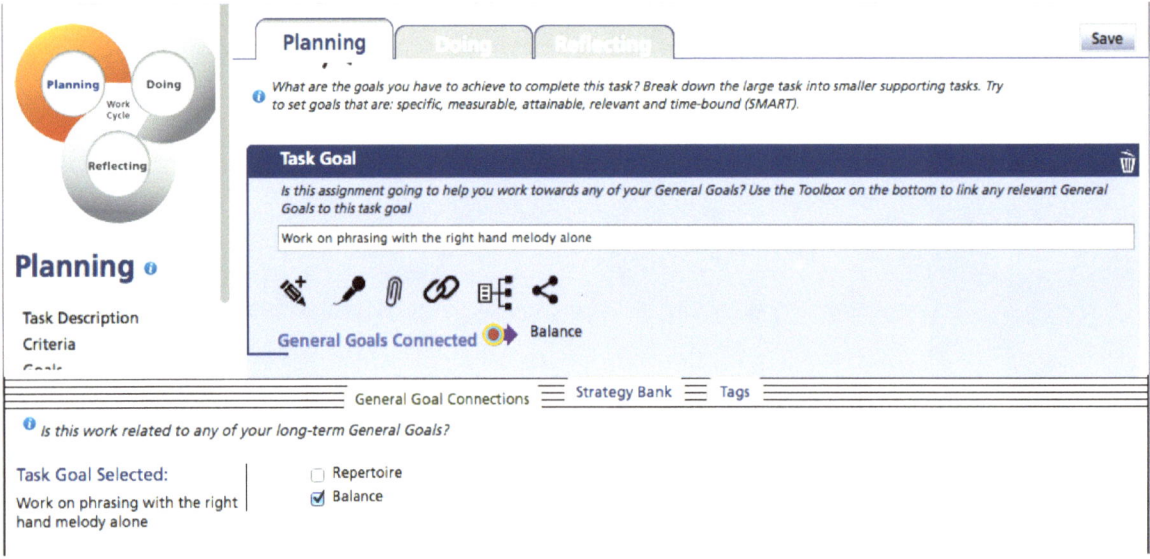

Tags

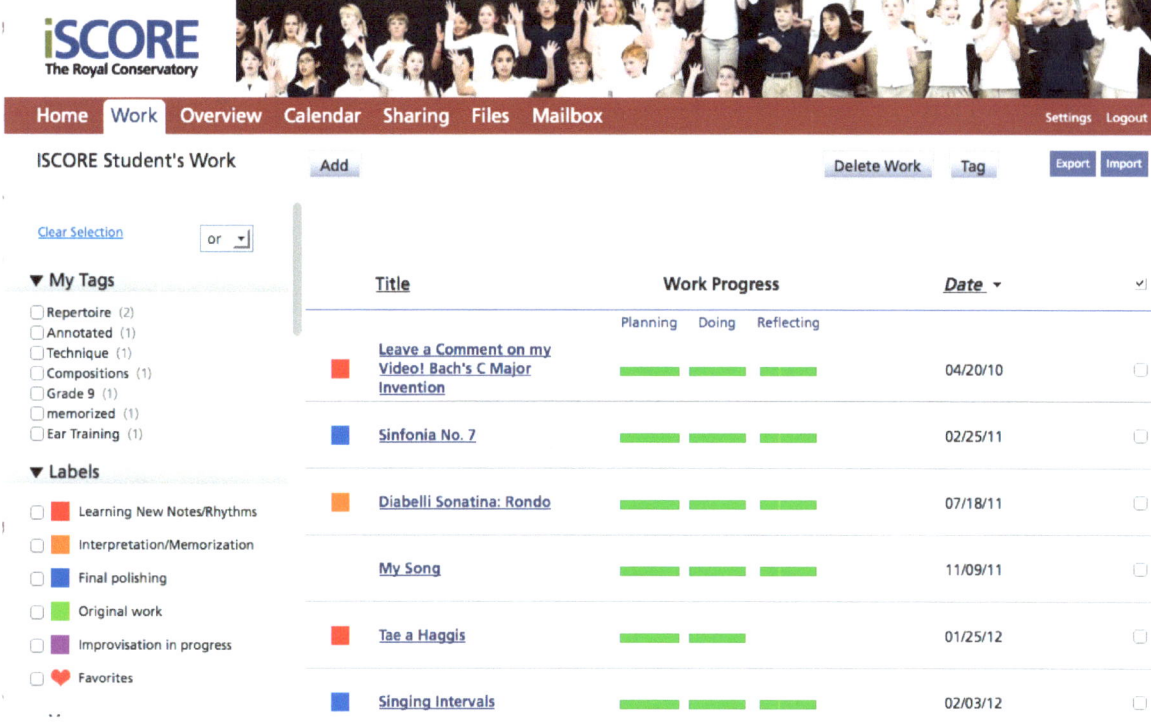

Use tags to label and organize your work. Tags will be added to the filter in your work index and can be reused. To link a tag to your work or to create a new tag:

1. Click on Work and select a project.
2. Click Add Tags. A text box will pop up.
3. Write in the box and then click Add.
4. Click on an existing tag and click Add to link it to your Work.
5. To edit a tag name, click on 🖉
6. To delete a tag from the Tags area, click on 🗑

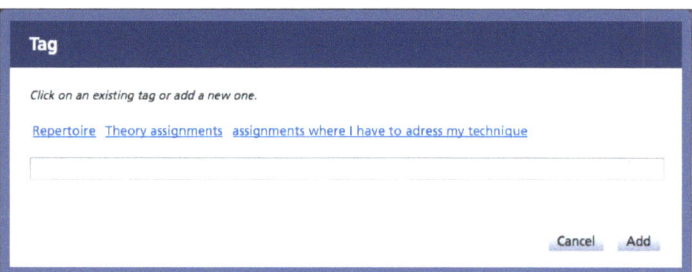

Schedule

Click on 🗓 to open the Calendar and schedule your work.

Motivation

Motivation is the reason you may or may not want to do something.

To describe your motivation:

1. Use the slide bar to rate how much you want to work on your task.

2. Click on ✏️ to describe how you will stay motivated

   or

3. Click on + Need help? Answer these: to answer the questions provided and use the slide bar.

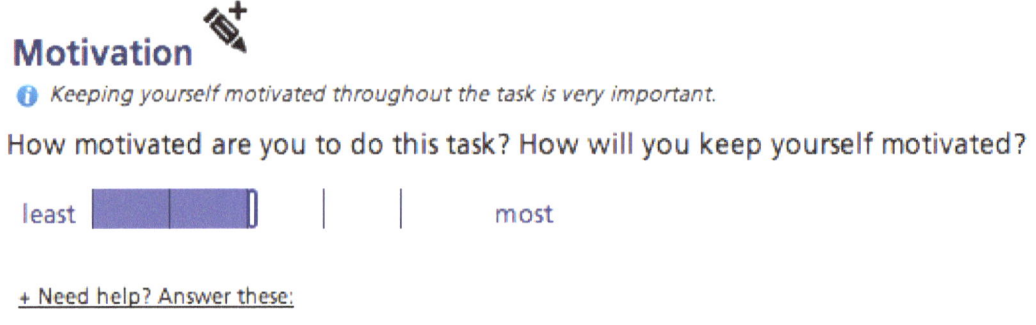

Saving

1. Click on Save at the top right corner to save your work.
2. To modify the date last saved, go to the work index page and adjust the date every time you edit your work by using:
3. You can also adjust the date started.

Detailed User Guide

Doing

This is where you will show your work using a combination of text, audio, and video. You can also post links to other performances and comment on how the links have influenced your learning. In the lower menu of the Doing page, there is a journal for reflections as you engage in your work.

Text Editor

Click on the  to write in the text editor.

Text
Please press the Save button when you are finished writing your text.

Write your text in this box after you've clicked on the Text Editor icon.

You can change the size, style, and colour of your font.

Audio Recorder

1. Click on ![mic] to audio-record your goal.
2. An Adobe Flash Player Settings Box will pop up and you need to click on ![Allow] so that the Audio Recorder can access your computer's microphone.

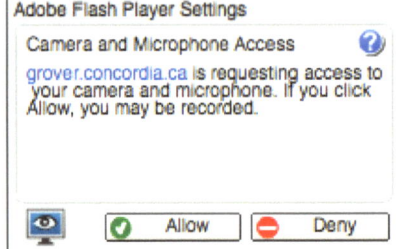

3. Click on the microphone ![mic] to start recording (the microphone will turn red).
4. Click on the microphone again to stop recording (the microphone will turn grey).
5. After the recording has converted and uploaded, click on the play button to listen to your recording.
6. Click on the Export button to download your recording as an MP3 file.

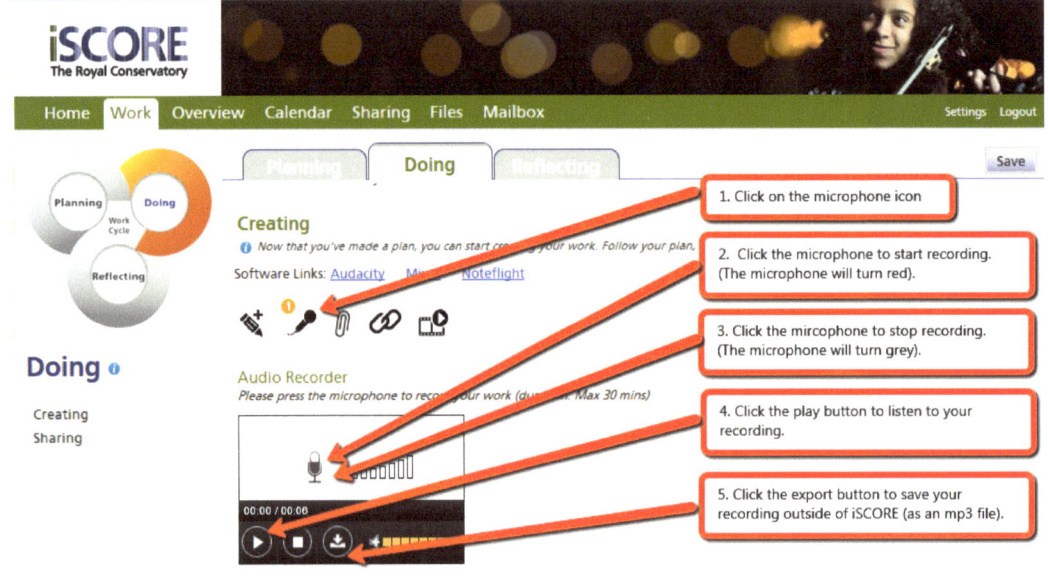

Attach a File

1. Click on
2. Click Browse to find the file from your computer or device.
3. Click Add to attach the file to your Work.

Paste a Link

1. Click on the 🔗
2. Copy URL address of the website.
3. Paste the URL address in the box.
4. Click ✓ to save link.

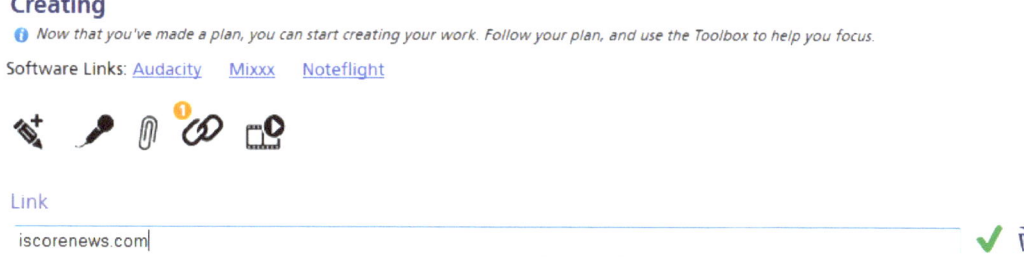

Uploading Media into Your *Teacher* Portfolio

1. Click on Work on the horizontal menu.
2. Select an existing work or create a new one.
3. Click on the Doing tab.
4. Click on the Media icon
5. Click on "Click to add media!" button.
6. Upload audio/video files from your computer.

Trouble-shooting tip: Sometimes videos need to be compressed before they can be uploaded successfully. For example, an AVI video could take hours to upload! Experiment with different video converters to see what works best on your system. Some students have had good experiences with Miro Video Converter (www.mirovideoconverter.com). It's free.

Uploading Media into Your *Student's* Portfolio

1. Access your student's portfolio through iSCORE Manage.
2. Click on Work on the horizontal menu.
3. Select a work.
4. Click on Doing.
5. Scroll to the bottom of the Doing page and Click on "Attach Media."
6. Click on Upload new media.
7. Upload audio/video files from your computer. You can now comment on the recording by annotating (see below).

Adding an Annotation to a Video/Audio Recording

1. Access your student's portfolio through iSCORE Manage.
2. Click on Work on the horizontal menu.

3. Select the title of the work you want to annotate.
4. Click on the Doing tab to access the recording.
5. Play the video/audio recording and pause it where you want to add an annotation.
6. Click on either ![icon] to make a text annotation, or ![icon] to record your annotation.

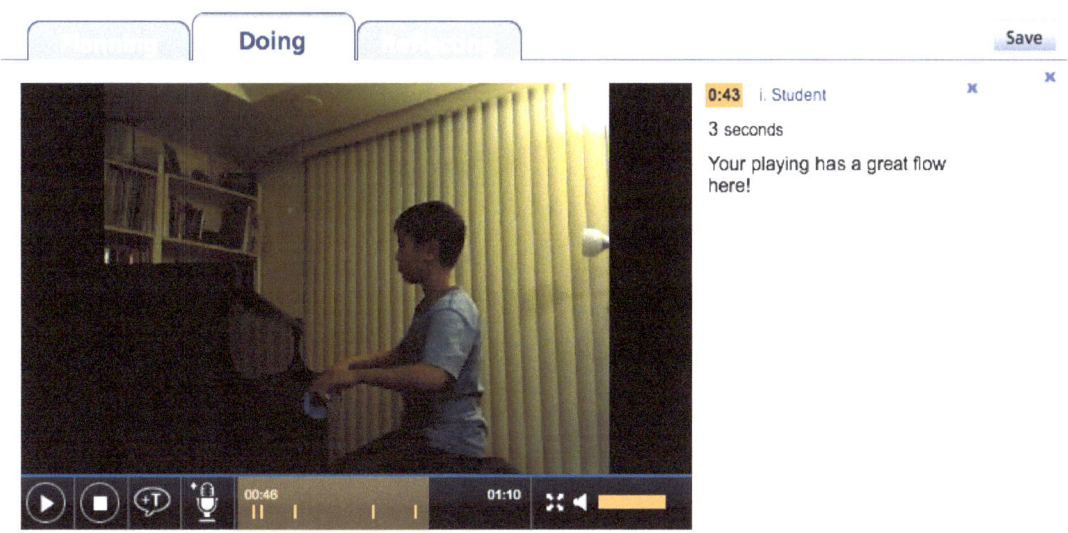

Adding a Text Annotation

1. Click on ![icon]
2. Type in the annotation text.
3. Choose how long you want the annotation to be displayed while the video is playing. The timing is important so that your intent is clear for the student.
4. Click on Save.

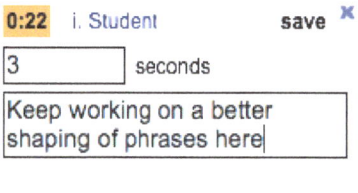

Adding a Recorded Annotation

1. Click on ![mic icon]

2. A red microphone icon will show up on the right side of the video.
3. Click on the red microphone icon to start the recording.
4. When you click on the red microphone icon, you will first see an Adobe Flash Player Settings window pop up, asking to access the computer's camera and microphone. In order for this feature to work, you must click on Allow.

5. The recording will start immediately.
6. When you are finished with your recording, click on the red stop button.

7. Remember to click on Save before leaving the page.

When playing a video or audio recording, the audio annotations pause the recording, whereas the text annotations are displayed while the recording is playing.

Connect to Other Software

You can also access other software that can help you create music.

1. Click on *Mixxx* to create a sequence of songs/pieces using this downloadable software.
1. Click on *Audacity* to record or edit your music using this downloadable software.
2. Click on *Noteflight* to create a score using this web-based software.

My Plan

Click here to review the goals your set in the Planning section.

Checklist

Your Strategies are listed here so that you can keep track of what you have done so far.

Click on the pencil icon to add your own observations of how the strategies are working out.

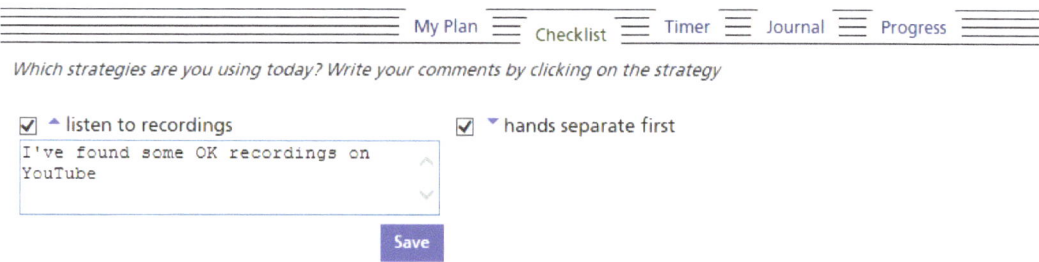

Timer

Use the timer to keep track of your time spent on a task.

1. Click **Start Timer** to start the timer.
2. Write what you are timing in the text box **Title**
3. Click **End Timer** to stop the timer.

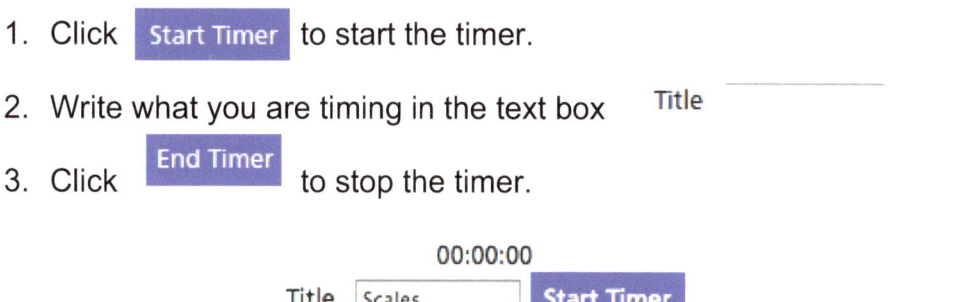

Note: As long as the timer is still running, a stopwatch icon will appear at the top of the page.

Journal

Write about your learning process to help you to stay on track with your musical tasks. You can also use the journal to note any changes that you would like to make along the way or to make note of recurring patterns.

1. Write in the text box.
2. Click Save when you are done writing.

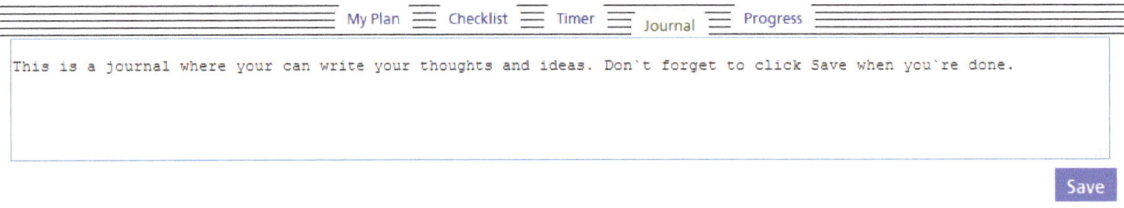

Progress

Your Task Goals and Supporting Task Goals are listed here with slide bars. Use these slide bars to mark your progress at any time in the learning process.

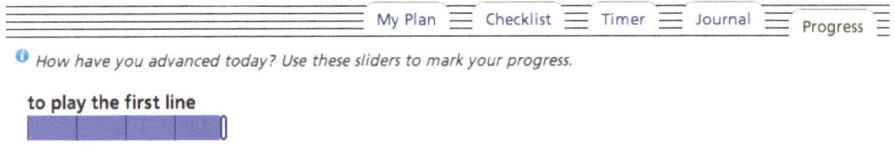

Reflecting

Click on the Reflecting tab to comment on your accomplishments with your project.

Self-Evaluation

Rate and describe how well you think you did.

1. Click on ✏️ to write your reflection using the text editor.
2. Click on 🎤 to audio-record your reflection.
3. Click on 📎 to attach a file to your reflection.
4. Click on 🔗 to create a link to your reflection.

For more assistance, click on "+ Need help? Answer these:"

You can also click on the bottom of your screen to review your Goals, Criteria, and Strategies from your Planning and Doing stages.

Click on Goals to review the progress you made on your task goals and Supporting Tasks in the Doing stage.

Click on Criteria to review the criteria you had set in the Planning stage.

Click on Strategies to review how much you used your strategies. Use the slide bar to mark the amount from least to most.

Cause

Why did the outcome meet or not meet your expectations? Explain in the text editor by clicking on

Satisfaction

Use the slidebar to rate how pleased you are with your work and outcome.

Lessons Learned

What new skills or learning habits did you gain? How can you use these new understandings to help you to work on a similar or related task next time? Explain by clicking on the   icon.

Saved Filters

You can view work in your work index through filters. These filters can be any of the labels or tags that you have created. You can also organize your work by grouping your labels and/or tags into saved filters.

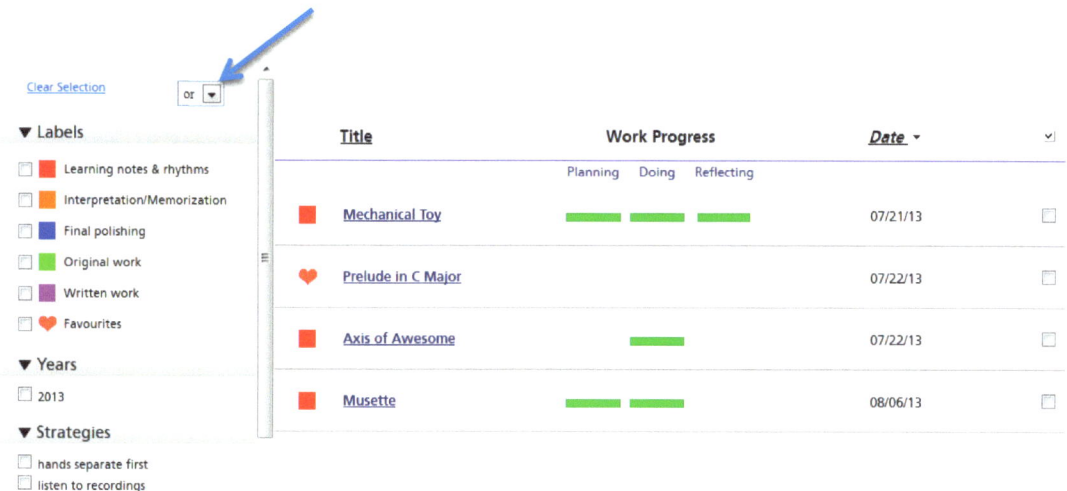

1. Scroll down the left side bar of the Work Index.
2. Select one or more of the labels or tags at the top right as shown.
3. The projects associated with these labels or tags will appear.

Overview

The "Overview" tab allows you to see how often you have been using different strategies and how often your work projects connect to your General Goals. You can also rename your strategies from this page, but you cannot add a strategy on the Overview page nor can you edit a strategy from here.

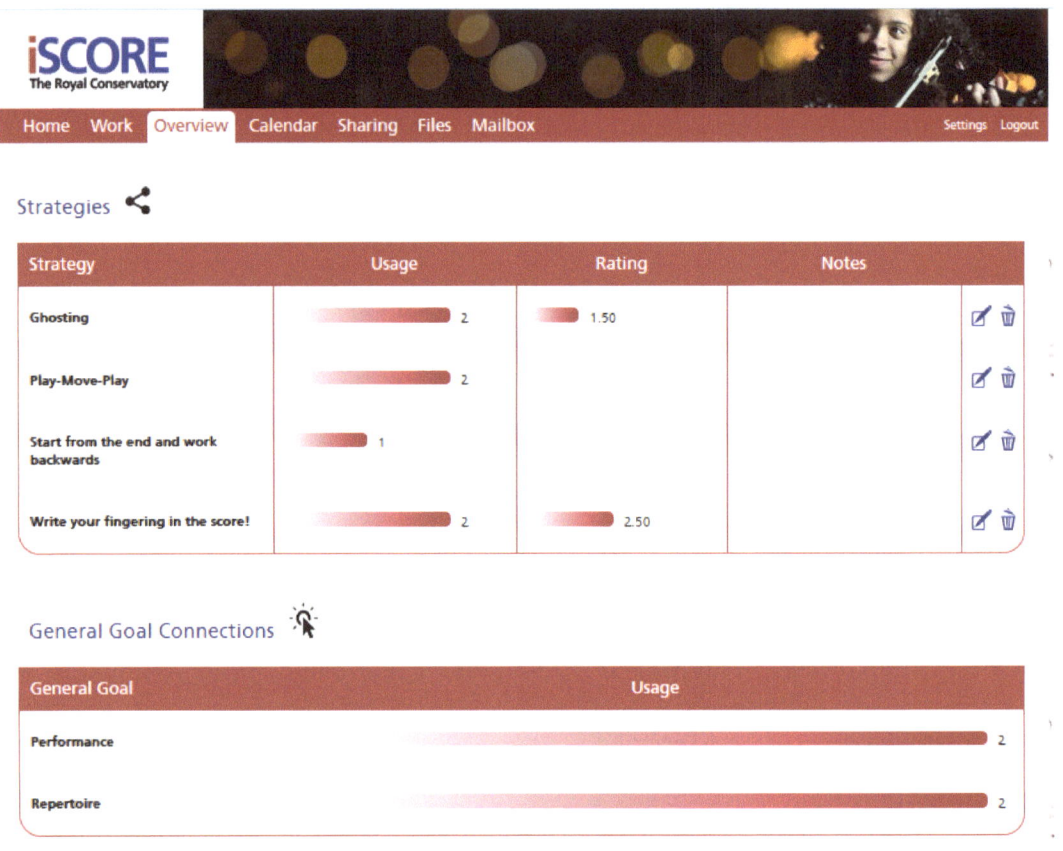

1. To rename a strategy click
2. To delete a strategy click
3. To create a strategy, go to the planning section of any project file, click task goal, and then select the strategy icon. Remember to save your strategy.

Calendar

Use the calendar to schedule rehearsals, lessons, or concerts.

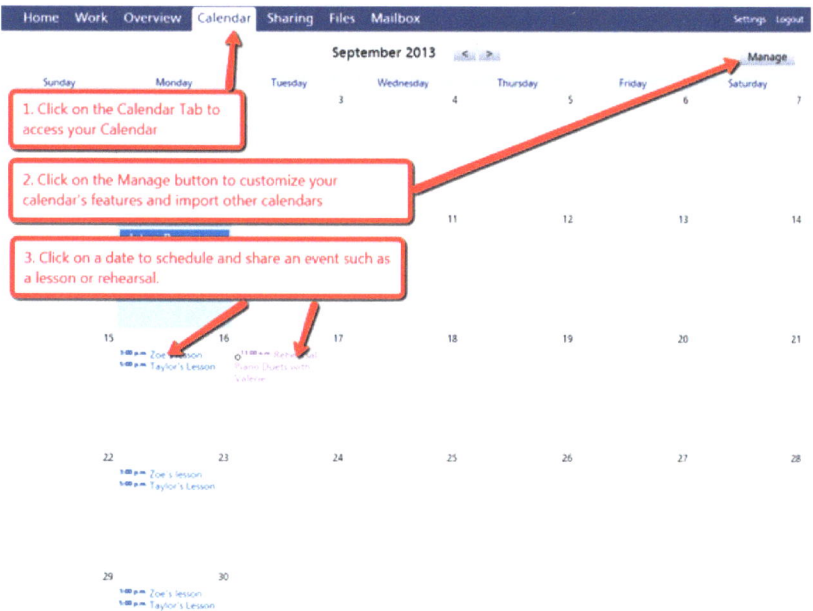

Creating Categories in Your Calendar

The **Manage My Calendar** section is where you can create different colour-coded categories to organize your events such as lessons, recitals, rehearsals, competitions, or exams.

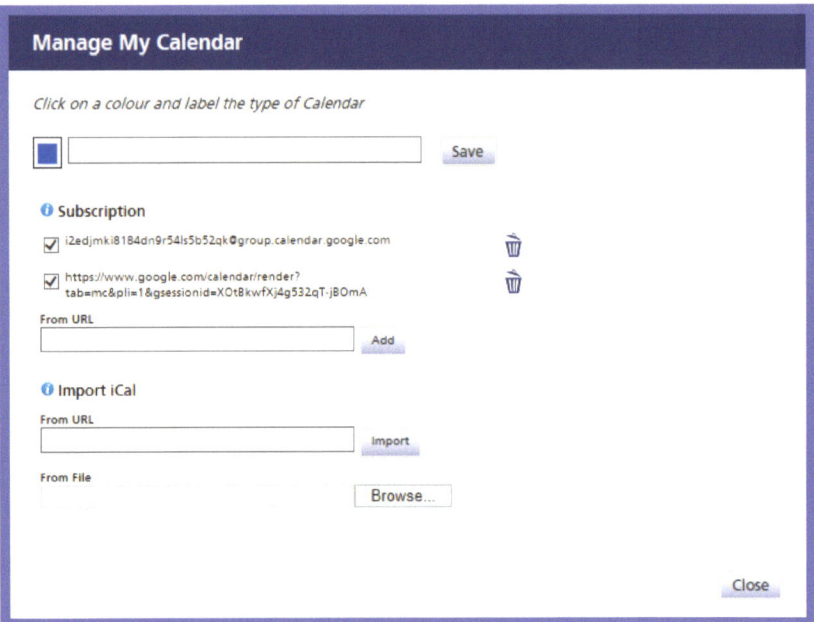

1. Access Manage My Calendar by clicking on the Manage button in the upper right-hand corner of the Calendar.

2. Click on the coloured square on the left side to bring up the column of colours to choose from.

3. Type the category name in the blank beside it and click Save.

4. Repeat as often as you would like and remember to save your choices; you are always free to change your choices later.

The Calendar is versatile; it can adapt to existing calendar applications.

1. If you subscribe to an online calendar, type the URL in the Subscription field and then click Add.

2. If you want to upload your iCal file from your computer, click on Browse to upload the filename or click on Import to provide the URL if you store it online.

Creating and Sharing Events in Your Calendar

Now that your event categories have been set, you can start to create and share events. When you create an event in your calendar, such as a lesson time slot or a recital, you can share this schedule with your whole studio or just selected students. This way, students or fellow teachers in your studio can see any lesson schedules, changes, or other events.

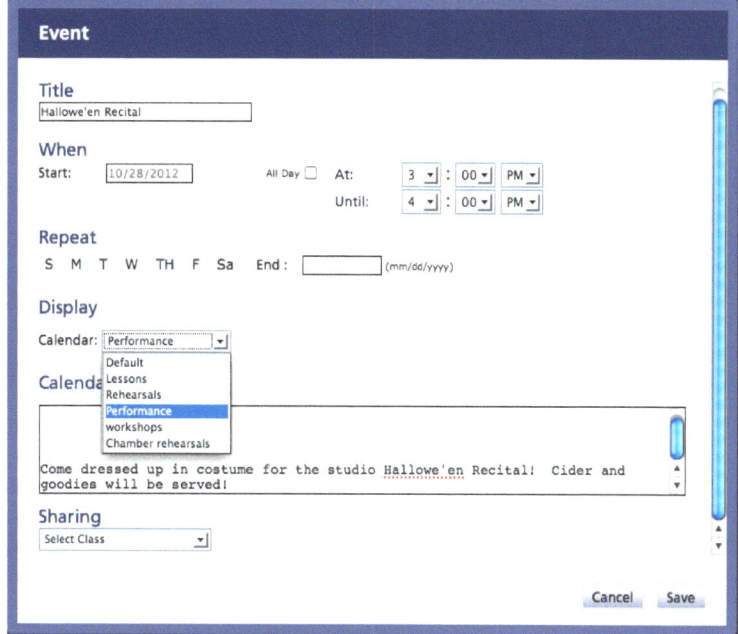

1. Click on any date on the Calendar where you want to schedule an event.
2. An Event page will pop up and you can enter the title of your event.
3. Uncheck the All Day box to specify a start and end time for your event.

4. Click on the day(s) you want this event to repeat (such as lesson times) and type in an end date if needed.
5. Click on the drop-down menu under Display to choose a category for this event. The colour you chose for the category in the Manage section will be the colour in which your event appears in the Calendar.
6. Type an event description in the Calendar Description box.
7. Click on the drop-down menu under Sharing to choose those with whom you want to share this event.
8. Remember to click on Save when you are finished!

Files

You can collect files and links in the File tab and/or share them for others to see. You can also view files that have been shared with you.

To Add a File

1. Click Add File.
2. Click on Choose File.
3. Add your file.
4. Click Save to upload it.

To Add a Link

1. Click Add Link.
2. Type in a title for your link and paste the URL.
3. Click Save.

Searching Your Files

My Files: Shows the Files you have uploaded.

All Files: Shows all the Files in the Filing Cabinet.

Files Shared With Me: Shows files shared with you.

Resources: Files developed by the iSCORE team for support.

Links: All the links in the Filing Cabinet.

Your files can be filtered by File type or Resource type. Click the box beside the desired type.

Sharing Your Files

Storing resources in your iSCORE Files allows you to store and share resources easily with your students.

From Files tab to Files tab: To share a link or file, allowing it to appear in another person's Files tab, do the following:

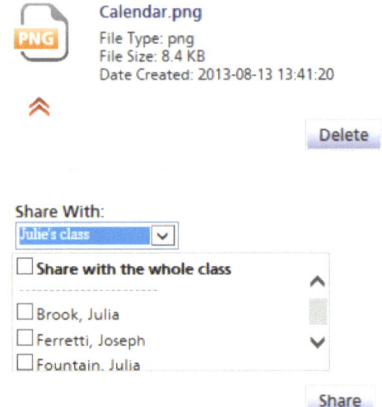

1. Click on the file icon ⌄ to open up the sharing feature.
2. Select the class and member of the class with whom you want to share the file in the pop-up drop-down menu and click on Share.
3. You may also share an item with the whole class.
4. These files will now appear in the person's Files tab.

Attaching Files with Notes & Posts or the Mailbox: Items in your Files tab can be attached in the Notes & Posts area on your home page. They can also be attached with messages in the iSCORE Mailbox. These features allow you to send and receive resources without having to clutter your own personal mail browser. To do so:

1. Click on Attach File.
2. Select the file you want to share.
3. Click on Add.

Sharing

The Sharing tab is where you view other students' work and where you grant permissions for others to see your home page and Work.

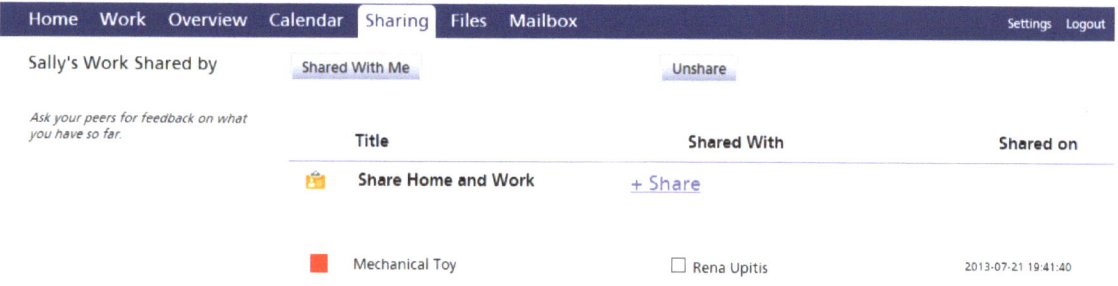

To share your Home and all your Work pages with other students and teachers:

1. Click +Share
2. Select a class from the drop-down menu.
3. Click on a box to share with a specific student or multiple students, or choose "Share with the whole class."
4. Click Share.

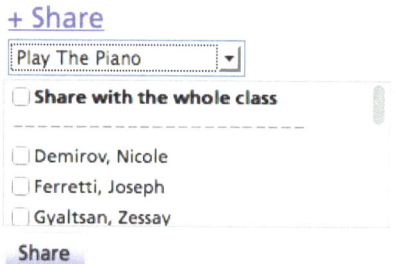

You can stop sharing individual Work pages that you have shared:

1. Check off the work you would like to stop sharing
2. Click on Unshare at the top of the page.

To see the portfolios that have been shared with you:

1. Click Shared With Me, and a list of people who have shared with you will appear.
2. Click the 👁 icon to see their work.

Sharing Calendar Events: Go to the section on Calendar (see p. 75).
Sharing Files: Go to the section on Files (see p. 78).
Note: You can choose the parts of your home page you want to share in Settings (see p. 51).

Viewing Student Portfolios from Sharing

You can also view your students' portfolios from within the Sharing tab of iSCORE.

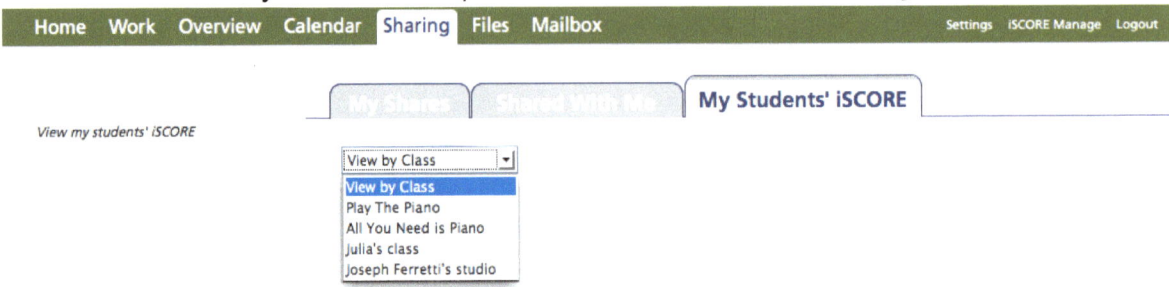

From the Sharing tab, click on "My Students' iSCORE" and select your class by clicking on the "View by Class" dropdown menu.
The list of students in the selected class will then display. Click on the 👁 beside the student portfolio you want to view.

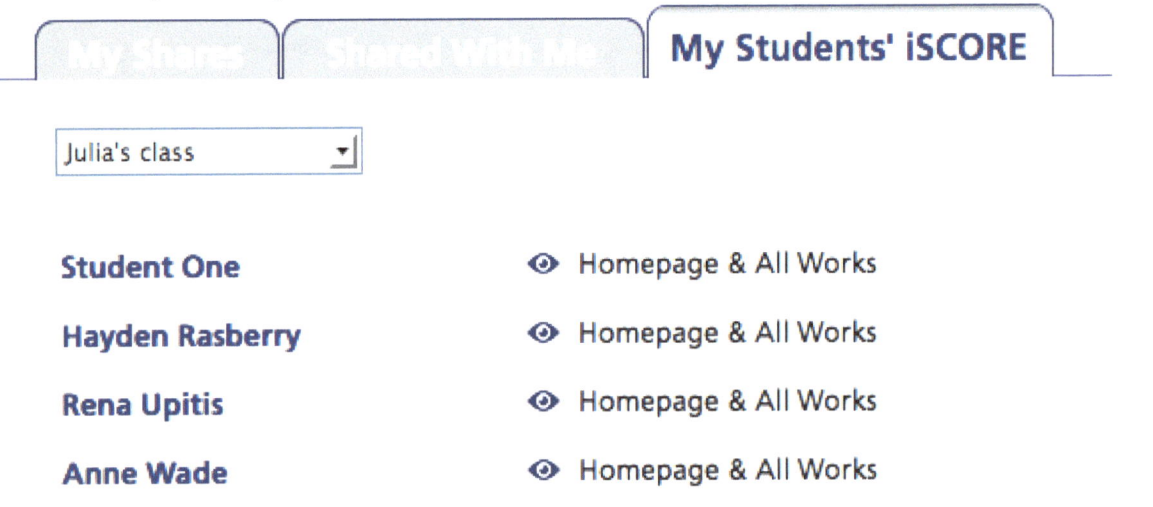

Mailbox

The mailbox is where you can send and receive messages.

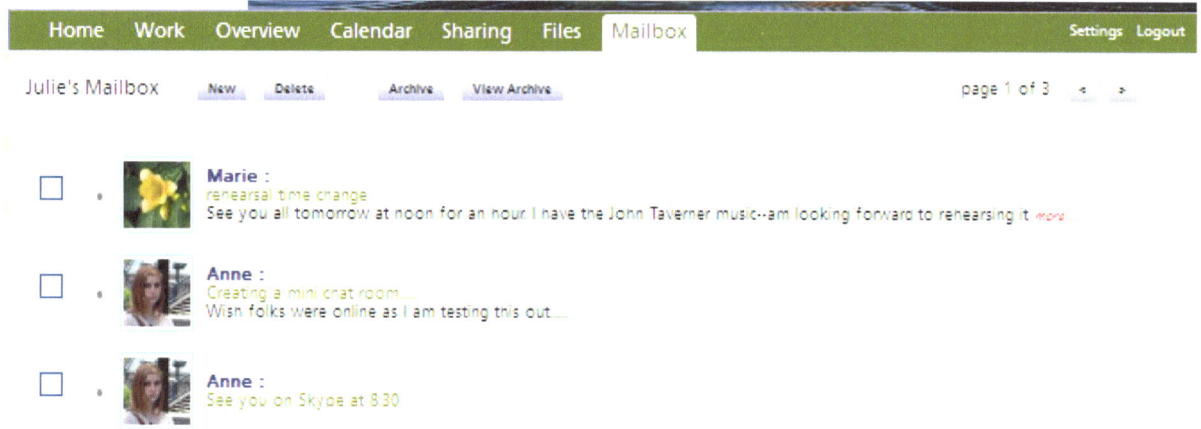

To write a message:

1. Click New.
2. A pop-up window will appear. Select the class the person is in. Then select the person or people to receive the message.
3. Write the subject of the message in the subject box and the message in the large box.

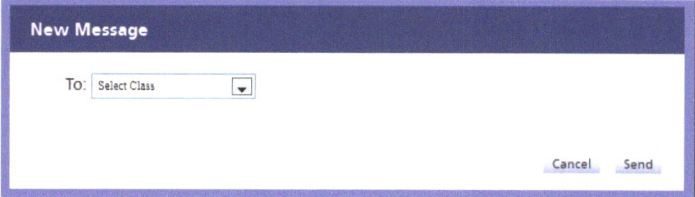

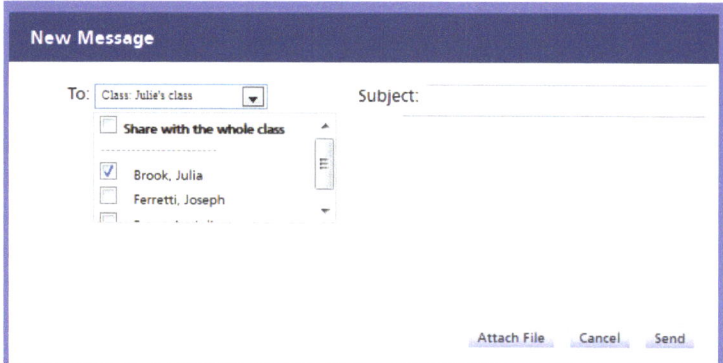

To attach a file to your message:

1. Click Attach File and select the file from your iSCORE Files.
2. Click Send.

To archive a message:

1. Select the message.
2. Click the Archive button.

To view the messages that you have archived, click on archived messages.

Delete a message by selecting the message and clicking Delete.

If the receiver is online at the same time as the sender, the Mailbox can become a chat syste

iSCORE iDEAS

Using the iSCORE Home Page as an Online Dictation Book

You can use the iSCORE home page as an online dictation book to record tasks and strategies. Students can also personalize their pictures and messages on the home page. By using the home page in this way, you can help students plan and reflect on their work.

Notes & Posts: As the teacher, you can write directly on your student's portfolio using Notes & Posts. You can type assignments, attach documents and audio or video files, and paste links to YouTube videos or websites. (Note that only documents already in iSCORE Files will be available to upload here.) To access your student's Notes & Posts:

1. Click on iSCORE Manage in the upper right-hand corner.
2. Scroll through your class list to find your student's portfolio.
3. Click on View Portfolio.

Similarly, the student can also upload his or her work to Notes & Posts and can attach a recording or a link. For example, students can record themselves and attach an MP3 version or a link to YouTube for their teachers, parents, or peers to listen to. When they complete their note, they could also describe what they liked about the recording or what their next steps will be. Here are the steps for the student who wants to share work through Notes and Posts:

1. Click on + and write your thoughts.
2. Click on Attach File to upload a document, audio, or video file from your filing cabinet.
3. Click on Post to display your message.

General Goals: Students can outline what they want to accomplish over the upcoming year in this area. Writing their goals will allow them to see how the tasks they complete each week are related to the general goals they have set.

1. Click on the +
2. Type a title/category for a goal and then describe the goal in the text box below.
3. Click on ✓ to save.
4. Click on ✎ to edit a goal or ✗ to delete a goal as needed.

To Do List: This is a place where students or teachers can outline the strategies they will need to use to accomplish their tasks, and the number of days they want to practice. We hope the process of typing the tasks will help students remember them!

1. Click on the +
2. Type the task(s).
3. Click on ✓ to save.
4. To edit a goal, click on ✎
5. Click on ✗ to delete a goal.

Using iSCORE to Compare Performances

Through iSCORE, you can compare performances in order to help students develop their listening skills. Recordings can either be uploaded files or links to YouTube.

1. Go to the Work tab.
2. Click Add to create a project to upload the different performances.
3. Click on the Doing section of the Project.
4. Click on the link icon to paste web links to various performances. To link to more than one performance, simply click again on the icon and paste another URL.
5. Click on the attachment icon to attach a video or audio file of a performance. To attach more than one file, click again on the icon and upload another document.
6. Students can write their comparisons using the text editor, which will open when they click on

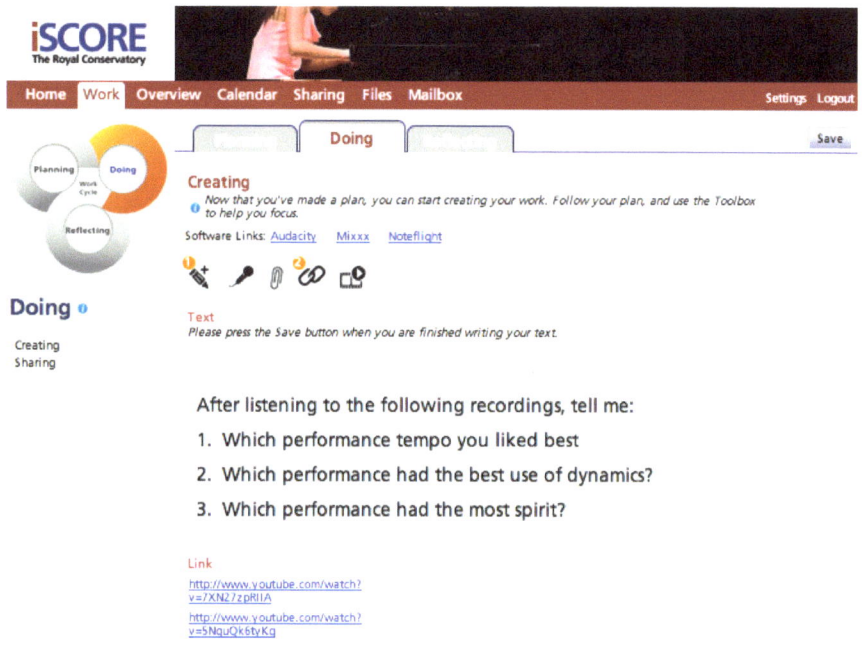

Using iSCORE to Compose

Many students enjoy composing their own music. iSCORE has features that can help students plan their compositions, capture their creations, and share them with peers, parents, and teachers.

Five ways to use iSCORE to improvise and compose

Recording is done through the Doing tab under Work, where students, their peers, teachers, or parents can later hear the composition and provide feedback on the work. Files can be attached to an iSCORE account by clicking on the paper clip and attaching the file.

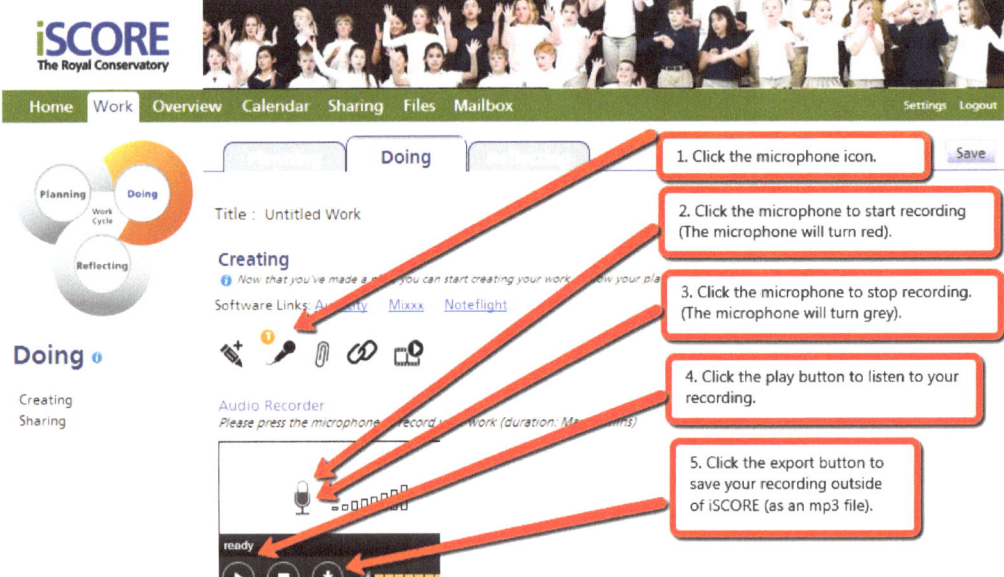

1. Audacity: This link will take students to the Audacity website, where they can download the Audacity software onto their computers. This software will let them record and edit sounds. Students can export their Audacity files as wav, MP3 or wma files and upload them to their iSCORE portfolios to share with peers and teachers. Audacity will let students add different layers onto their compositions. Students can also import recordings and edit them in Audacity.

2. Mixxx: This link will take students to the website where they can download the Mixxx software onto their computers. Students can use this software to help reinforce concepts of structure or sequence music, just as DJs do. Here are some creative assignments: 1) create a medley, making sure that all chosen excerpts share something in common (i.e., tempo, key, style, message); 2) create one unified piece in ABA form out of two separate pieces of music. Students can import their final creations into iSCORE for further reflection or sharing.

3. Noteflight: This link will take students to a website where they can sign up for a Noteflight web-based account. The free version of the account will allow students to keep up to 10 scores. Students can store these scores online, so they can retrieve them from any computer. Students can also export files in pdf format and store them in iSCORE. In addition, students can use Noteflight to write out their theory or harmony assignments. Teachers can use Noteflight to notate technical exercises.

4. Audio Recorder: Students can click on the microphone to record a performance of their own compositions. iSCORE will save these files. Students can export their recordings as MP3 files so that they can share them with others. For example, they can record their compositions and export the file to share with family.

5. Mobile devices: Some students will be so familiar with mobile devices that they will choose to record their compositions on the hand-held tools they carry in their pockets! Once the student has made a recording on a mobile device, the recording can be imported into iSCORE on the Doing section of the Work area. After importing the composition into iSCORE, the student can comment on the work, reflecting on the degree to which the composition meets expressive or communicative goals of the work, and plan the next creation.

OK, so how do they get started?

Planning: Suggest that students set a task goal before starting their compositions. What do they hope to accomplish? Encourage them to look back at their general goals. Will the task goal help them achieve one of their general goals?

Doing: Students might experiment with improvisations over chord patterns (e.g., play the bass notes of I, IV, V, I in any key, and add a melody overtop, exploring sounds that they like). Or more advanced students may select riffs to incorporate in jazz solos, developing strategies to improve their ability to play common chord patterns by ear. Once students are ready, they can record their work.

Reflecting: Encourage students to upload their compositions and share their artifacts with friends, talking about how their creations could be improved. Then have students incorporate these ideas into their next plan. If they are amenable, you could ask students to spend some time reflecting on what they have accomplished. Did their composition match their original intentions? What would they do differently the next time? As learners, what lessons about themselves will they take away from this?

Couldn't students just start by doing?

Yes. Many students will want to "jump right in" and begin working on musical ideas directly on their instruments. This is possible with iSCORE, as students can record the music as they develop it. Then they can play back melodic fragments, and reflect on what they like and what they'd like to change, and plan revisions.

Twist–Creating a Medley: Students might plan a particular type of composition—such as a medley of favourite Beatles tunes or tunes on the charts.

1. Students could use the Journal on the Doing Page to list the songs they want to incorporate.
2. They could paste a link to these songs in the Doing page (click on the link icon for each link or the paperclip to attach a file).
3. They could import these tracks into *Mixxx, Audacity*, or *Garage Band* and then explore how the sounds might fit together.
4. Using the Journal, they could think about what the tunes might have in common (e.g., tempo, key, style, and/or message) and then use iSCORE to create the medley. These medleys are great to share with friends and family.

Some highly motivated students might create a whole series of compositions, reflecting on the kinds of musical elements that they used successfully in their early works.

Using iSCORE to Practise

iSCORE can help foster better practice habits. Improved focus, faster goal attainment, and heightened awareness of technical and artistic elements are all areas that can be sharpened using the tool's various applications. The iSCORE *Work* tab outlines three distinct phases of the work process: Planning, Doing, and Reflecting. The Planning section provides a series of steps to help students think about what they need to do to be successful. The Doing section provides tools that allow students to document their work, and the Reflecting section poses questions that ask students to self-assess their work.

Ultimately, iSCORE encourages students to become more independent in their learning. They can choose which components they want to use in each section.

Planning

Take a look at the sample Planning page below.

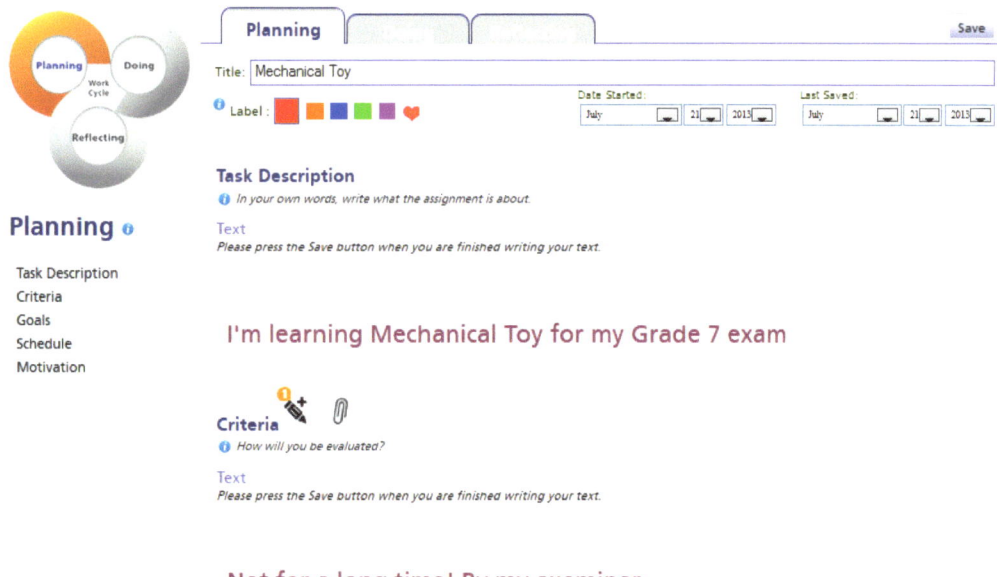

When on the Planning page, scroll down further to see:

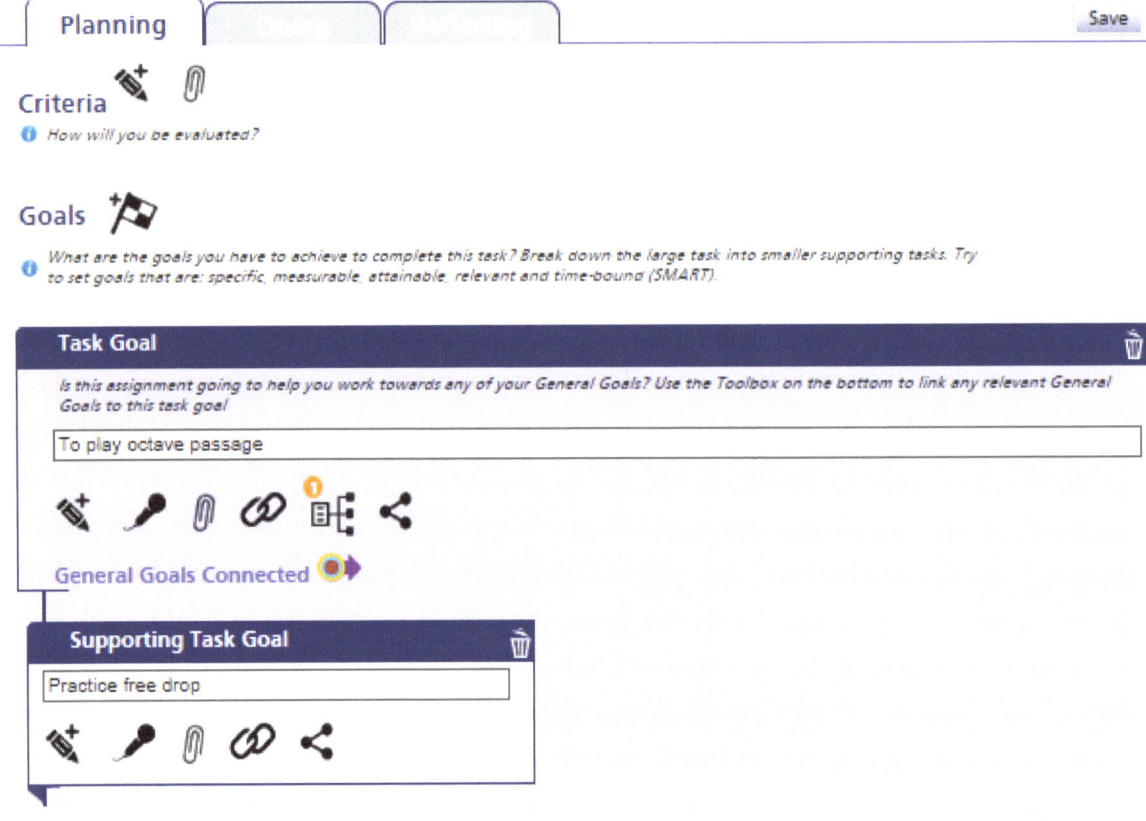

To create a Planning page:

1. Click on the Work tab on the home page.

2. Click on Add

3. Click on the icon next to Task Description and input a description of the project.

4. Click on the next to Criteria to type in a list of ideal results and qualities.

5. Click on the next to Goals and begin to set Task Goals. Students can enter numerous task goals.

Notice that in the example above, *Supporting* Task Goals and Strategies have been entered as well:

1. Click on ![icon] to enter a Supporting Task Goal. You can enter more than one.
2. Click on ![icon] to enter a Strategy. Again, you can enter numerous strategies.

Remember to click on Save after inputting any text! The Save icon is immediately to the right of the box where you enter your strategies. Note that saving the page itself will not save your strategies!

Some other useful features on the Planning page:

1. Click on the ![icon] to go directly into your calendar and schedule practice sessions.[1]
2. Click and drag your cursor along the Motivation bar to express the level of desire for this accomplishment.

Now that the student has created a plan, the core of the practising can be tracked and developed on the Doing page.

---

[1] For further information see "iSCORE iDEA—Using your Calendar" at www.iscorenews.com.

Doing

Below is the Doing tab of a sample Work project:

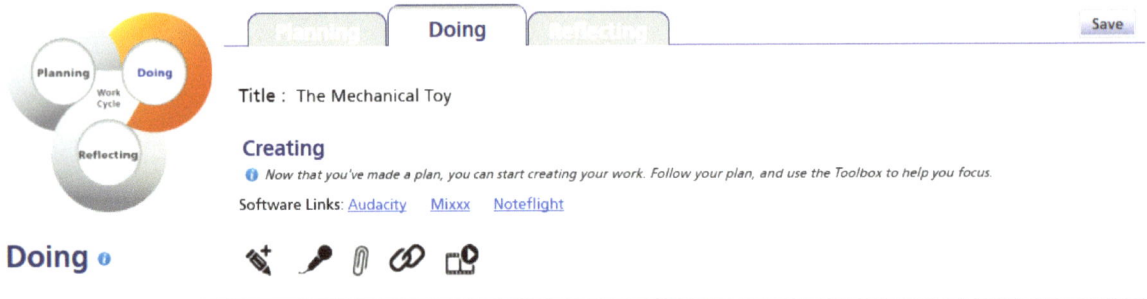

The Creating section of the Doing page offers the use of a text editor ( ), an embedded recording device ( ), and the option of attaching a file ( ), or attaching a link ( ).

The media box is a particularly useful tool for practising. Videos or recordings of projects in progress can be uploaded. They can be annotated by students, friends, teachers, and parents.

The Journal function is another particularly useful application on the Doing page that can be used to enhance practice results.

Click on the journal tab 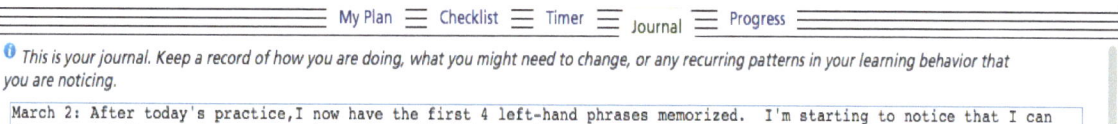 located on the tab bar at the bottom of the Doing page.

Begin to type a journal entry. When finished, remember to click on Save!

```
My Plan   Checklist   Timer   Journal   Progress
```
ⓘ *This is your journal. Keep a record of how you are doing, what you might need to change, or any recurring patterns in your learning behavior that you are noticing.*

```
March 2: After today's practice, I now have the first 4 left-hand phrases memorized.  I'm starting to notice that I can
flow through the melody more smoothly.  It really helps to have the notes in my head and fingers.  I can focus on
staying free and really hearing and blending the tones smoothly.  I'm trying to shape the phrases, but am finding that
it often sounds bumpy when I reach the high points.  Tomorrow I'll try being more continuous in my movements through the
long tones and see if that works.  If not, I'll see what advice Mrs. Doe might have for me on Thursday.  Hopefully I'll
get two more phrases down tomorrow.
```

Reflecting

The third and final tab of the Work project is the Reflecting page, which can help synthesize developments in practising.

The first application on your Reflecting page is the Self-Evaluation box. Click on the ✎ to type in a summary of your process.

The example on the following page illustrates that there are also icons available that allow you to record a verbal summary, attach a document, or create a link to a site that may contain your summary.

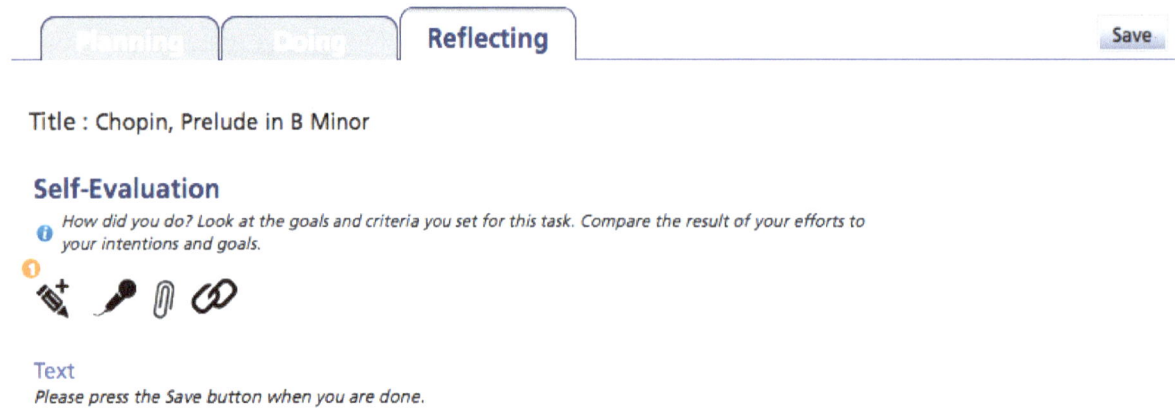

The Reflecting page also offers the chance to speculate on causes that may have contributed to your final results.

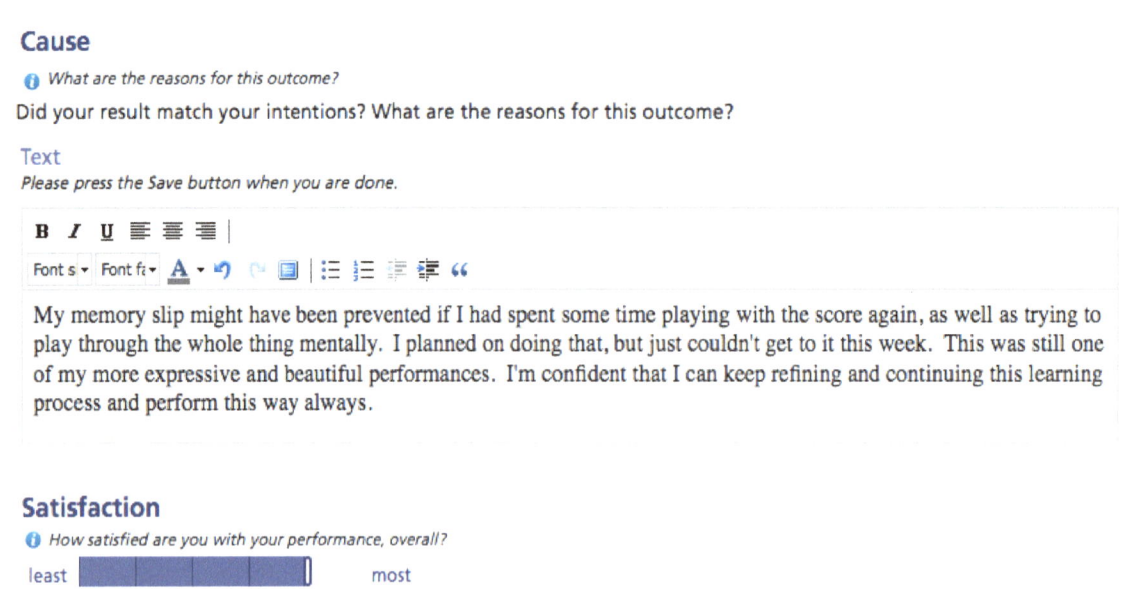

You can articulate Lessons Learned, which will shape the way you practise for your next project.

Lessons Learned

What can you do differently next time you approach a similar task? What are the lessons you will take away from this about yourself as a learner?

Text
Please press the Save button when you are done.

1) I will make more of a point to solidify memory with the methods above.

2) I will learn the rest of my pieces as conscientiously as I learned this one.

iSCORE offers an abundance of tools that can enhance practice quality. There are even more features in the Planning, Doing, and Reflecting tabs than those outlined here. Enjoy the many features even outside of the Work section of the tool that can enhance practising!

Using iSCORE to Help With Ear Training

Practising ear training exercises—identifying intervals, clapping rhythms, or playing back melodies aurally—is difficult for students to do alone.

Using the Annotation feature along with the Sharing capability of iSCORE, students can help one another with their ear training. Here are some steps you can take to help students practise their ear training:

1. Have a student record the following[1]:
    a. A series of intervals.
    b. A short rhythm (that is clapped or played).
    c. A short melody.

2. Save these recordings onto a computer.

3. Upload these recordings into the iSCORE Annotator ( )
    a. Go to Work.
    b. Click on Add to create a new artifact.
    c. Click on Doing.
    d. Click on the Annotator icon
    e. Click on "Click to Add Media!"
    f. Upload your saved recording.

---

[1] The teacher can also create a series of exercises to upload directly to the Annotator on the student's Doing page.

4. Now your Ear Training exercise is ready to share with a peer. To do this:
    a. Scroll to the bottom of the screen.
    b. Select a class to share with.
    c. Select a particular student to share with.
    d. Click Share.

5. To answer the Ear Training Questions:
    a. Go to Sharing.
    b. Click Shared With Me.
    c. Click on the name of the student who created the file.
    d. Click on View Portfolio.
    e. Play the annotation.
    f. After you hear the sample, click the Recorder icon to record your performance of the rhythm or melody.
    g. Play back the whole recording to hear the original rhythm/melody and your response.
    h. If desired or needed, continue making recordings until the original example and response match.

Using iSCORE for Student Communication

Powerful Pairs

Pair students of varying skill levels and ask them to critique each other's work using the Share feature.

Example Hunt

Do you have more than one student who is learning the same piece? Use the Mailbox to start a conversation with those students. Encourage them to post examples of performances of the piece (e.g., YouTube links). Then ask them to compare performances (see iSCORE iDEA on Comparing Performances, p. 89).

A Wish and a Star

Ask students to select a work of their own to comment on. Ask them to describe one element of the performance they like (a star) and one element they want to improve (a wish). Using the Share feature, have your students share their work with their peers. Ask all of them to give a "star" on their peer's work, and perhaps a "wish" as well.

Match-Up

Use the Mailbox to post a piece of music to the studio and challenge students to find another piece that is similar in some aspect (e.g., mood, tempo, theme, genre…). With the post, have students explain how the pieces are similar.

Help your students provide feedback with these tips:

1. Start with something positive (a "star").
2. Give concrete suggestions about how to improve the performance (a "wish").
3. Share a strategy that works for you.
4. Be honest.

Your fellow musicians will appreciate your insights to help improve their skills and performances!

Encouraging Communication Between Students and Parents: A Guide for Teachers to Share with Parents[4]

Watching your child grow...

Every day your child grows, but no one can see that growth on a daily basis. We usually see growth in hindsight—as we mark the annual notches on the door frame, or catch sight of a photo from the year before, or notice that clothes no longer fit.

The fact that it's hard to see growth is what makes it hard for children to appreciate their progress in music as well. Learning a piece of music takes a long time, and students may feel they aren't getting anywhere. This can be discouraging.

iSCORE offers wonderful opportunities for you and your child to see and hear musical progress on a daily or weekly basis.

Many students record themselves as a way of helping them refine their playing. The iSCORE embedded audio recorder provides easy access to an audio recorder and allows students to store their recordings for a particular piece in one place. One of the benefits of this feature is that you and your child can listen to past recordings and hear first-hand how your child's musical skills have changed.

---

[4] Teachers may want to hand this guide out to parents. There is a downloadable PDF version of this iSCORE iDEA on the website at www.iscorenews.com

To use iSCORE in this way...

  a. Log in to your child's portfolio.
  b. Click on Work.
  c. Select a piece from the Work list.
  d. Click on Doing.
  e. Play each of the audio and/or video recordings and listen carefully.

After you have listened to the recordings together, you and your child can discuss the biggest changes that you hear. You can ask your child about what changes were surprising, and the improvements that made him or her feel the most proud. It's a way of helping you see and hear your child grow—right before your eyes and ears!

STUDENT EXEMPLARS

The Home Page

Two sample home pages by students appear below and on the following page. Watch www.iscorenews.com for new examples. Every fall and winter there is a contest for students to enter their home page and the winning home pages are permanently displayed on the website.

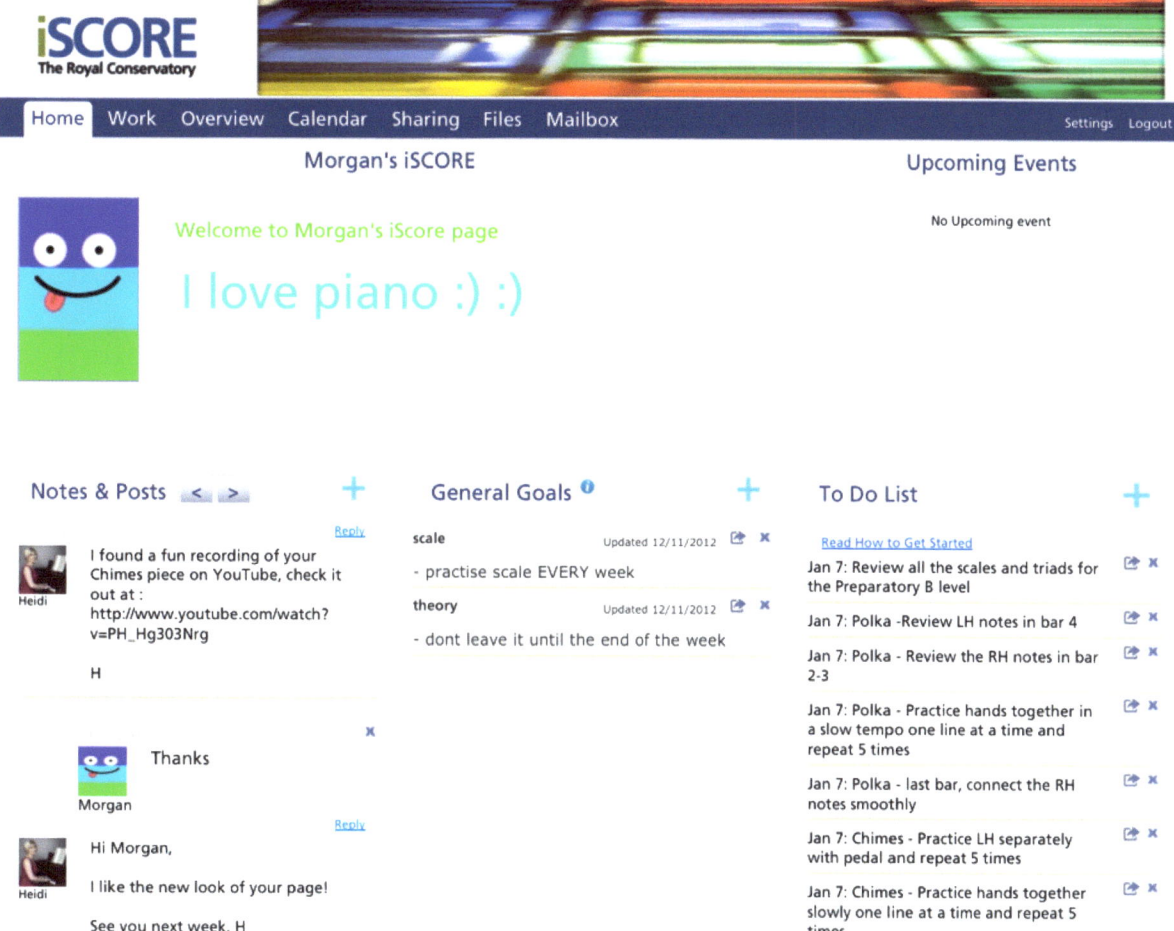

Work: Planning, Doing, & Reflecting

This section contains exemplars of students' plans and reflections on various aspects of their music study—learning new repertoire, composing, and practising familiar repertoire. The exemplars are illustrated with a variety of screen shots of the work in progress. The last example, *Bagatelle* (see p. 122), shows how parts of a project would appear as an exported work, when the student is ready to archive the work or to share it with teachers, parents, and peers.

More exemplars are regularly posted on www.iscorenews.com. Every fall and winter there is a contest for students to showcase their work, and the winning examples are permanently displayed on the website.

Using iSCORE to Learn a Piece: *Mouse in the Coal Bin*

This exemplar focuses only on the planning part of the self-regulated learning cycle, written by a young student. The student has written a task description in simple but clear terms, as well as criteria for evaluation and goals (task goal, supporting task goal, and strategies). The student has also indicated that she is motivated to learn the piece well enough to record it for her teacher.

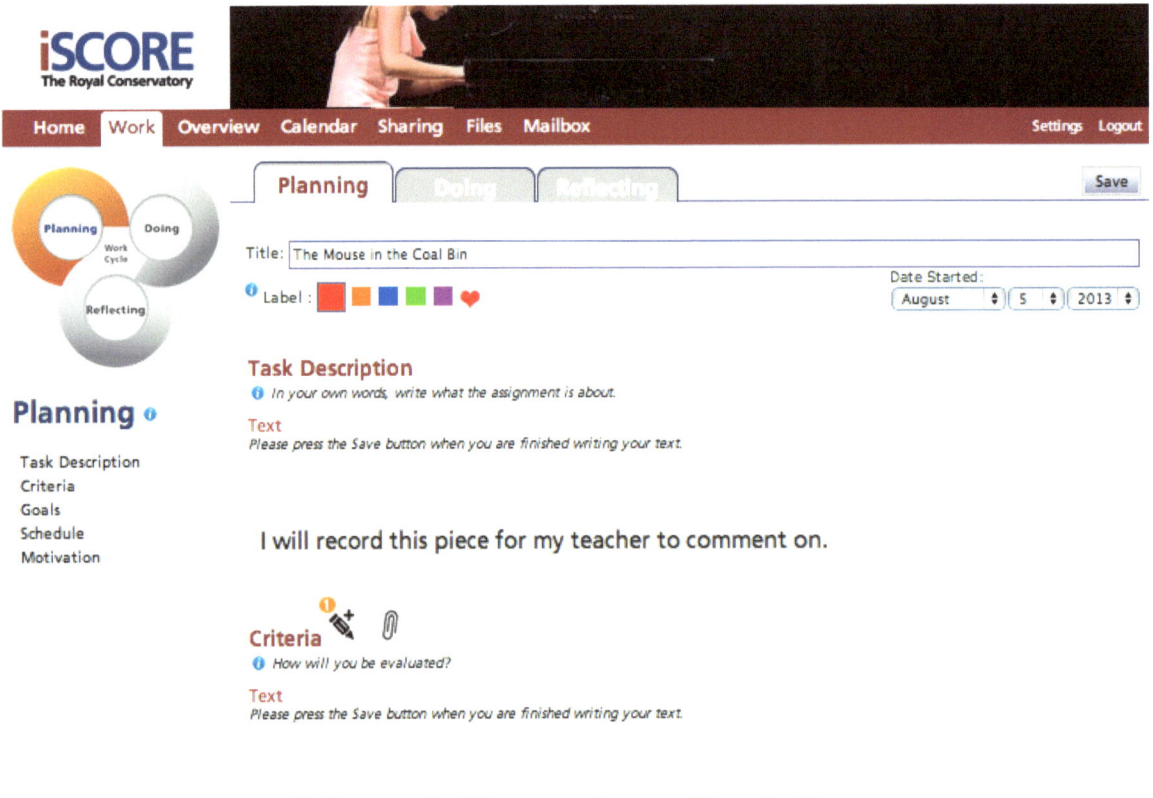

Goals

What are the goals you have to achieve to complete this task? Break down the large task into smaller supporting tasks. Try to set goals that are: specific, measurable, attainable, relevant and time-bound (SMART).

Task Goal

Is this assignment going to help you work towards any of your General Goals? Use the Toolbox on the bottom to link any relevant General Goals to this task goal

to play the second part without mistakes

General Goals Connected

Supporting Task Goal

Work on the second part by itself

Strategies

What processes or actions will direct you towards your goal? Select or add your learning strategies

Work in one bar bits

Schedule

Use the calendar to schedule your items.

Motivation

Keeping yourself motivated throughout the task is very important.

How motivated are you to do this task? How will you keep yourself motivated?

least [■■■■] most

+ Need help? Answer these:

Using iSCORE to Learn a Piece: *Prelude in B minor*

In the model below, the student has used the planning tab to write a task description and to state the criteria for judging the musicality of the performance of the piece. On the following page, the planning continues. Here the student has filled in a task goal, supporting tasks, and strategies that will guide his/her practice.

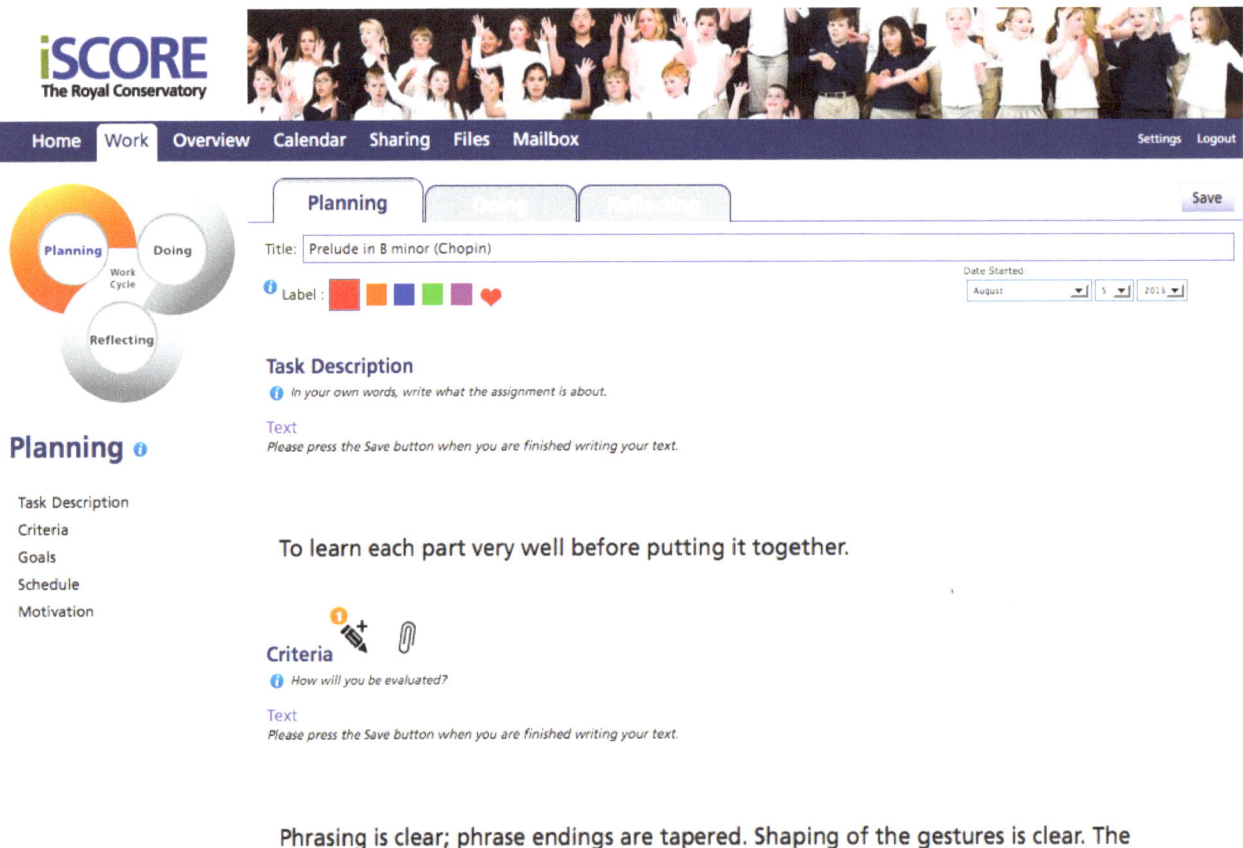

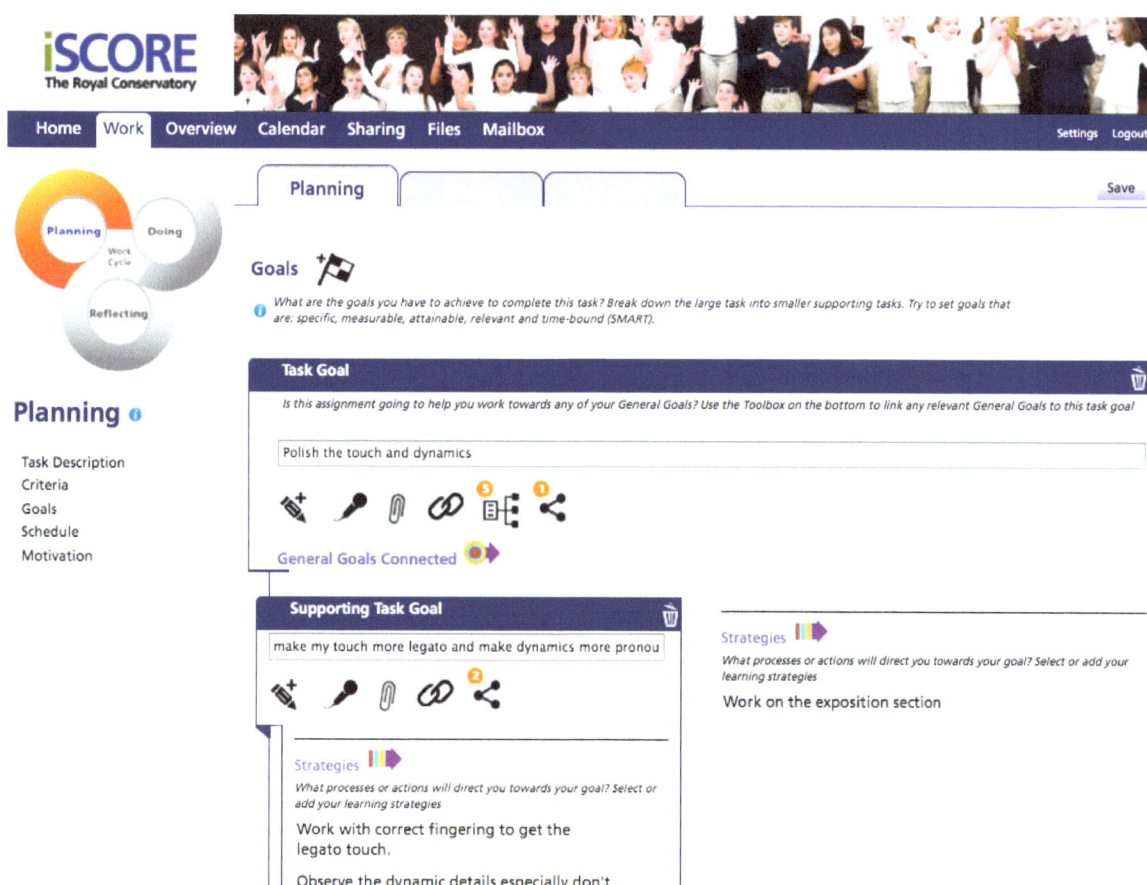

After completing the planning tab, the student moved to the doing tab and uploaded a video, using the media icon in the creating section of the page. The teacher has annotated this video where the vertical yellow bar appears.

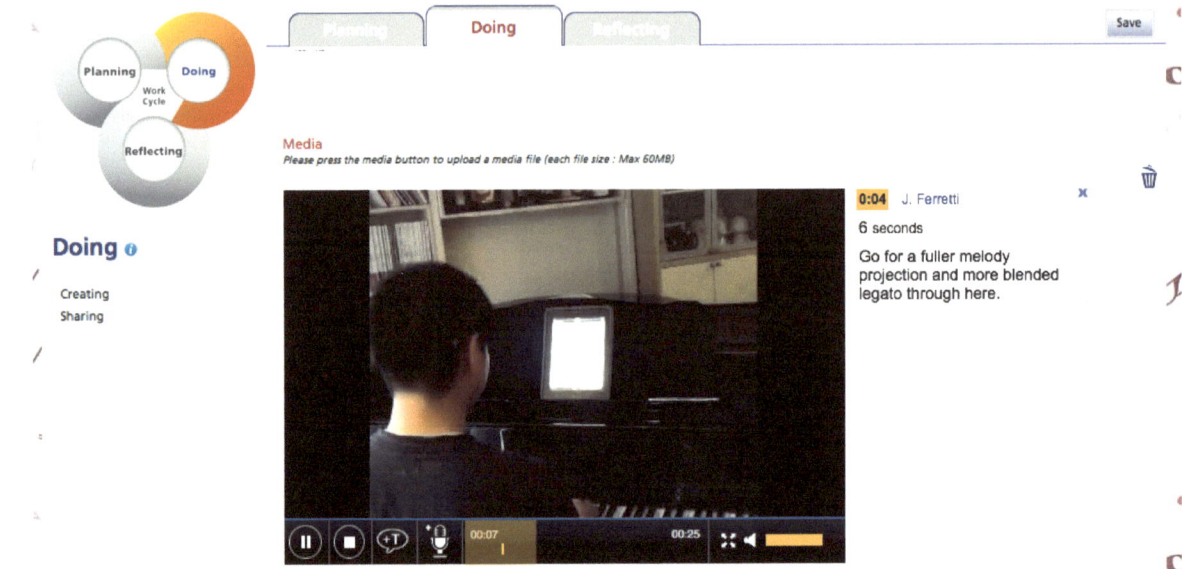

On the reflecting tab, the student has commented on the process of learning to play *Prelude in B minor*. Since this is still a work in progress, some of the comments are about ways that the student will continue to improve the work in the next planning-doing-reflecting cycle.

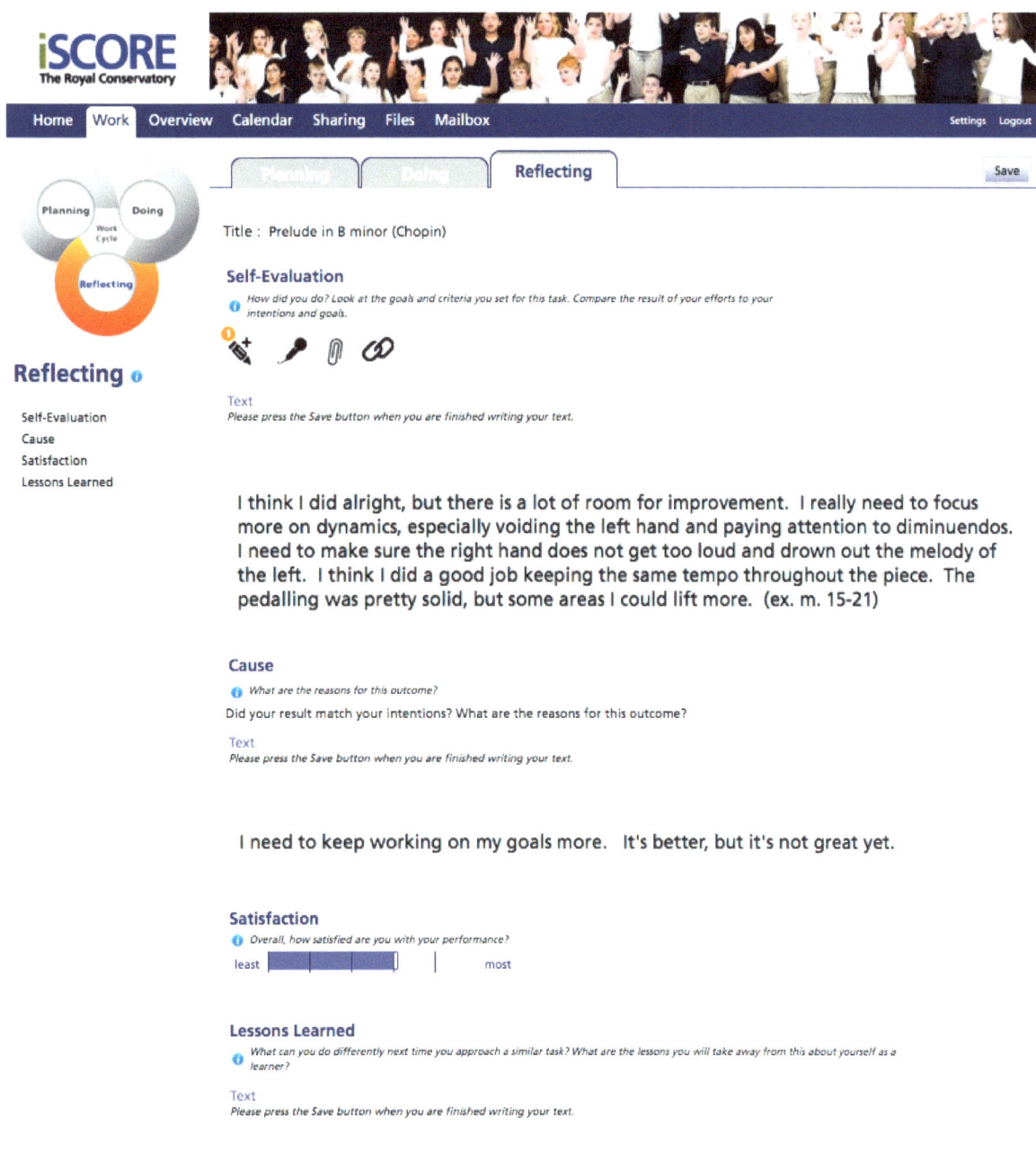

Using iSCORE to Learn a Piece by Ear: *The Scientist*

This exemplar shows how an intermediate student used iSCORE to learn a popular piece by ear. The student has filled out portions of the planning page as shown below, and on the following page the student's reflections are shown.

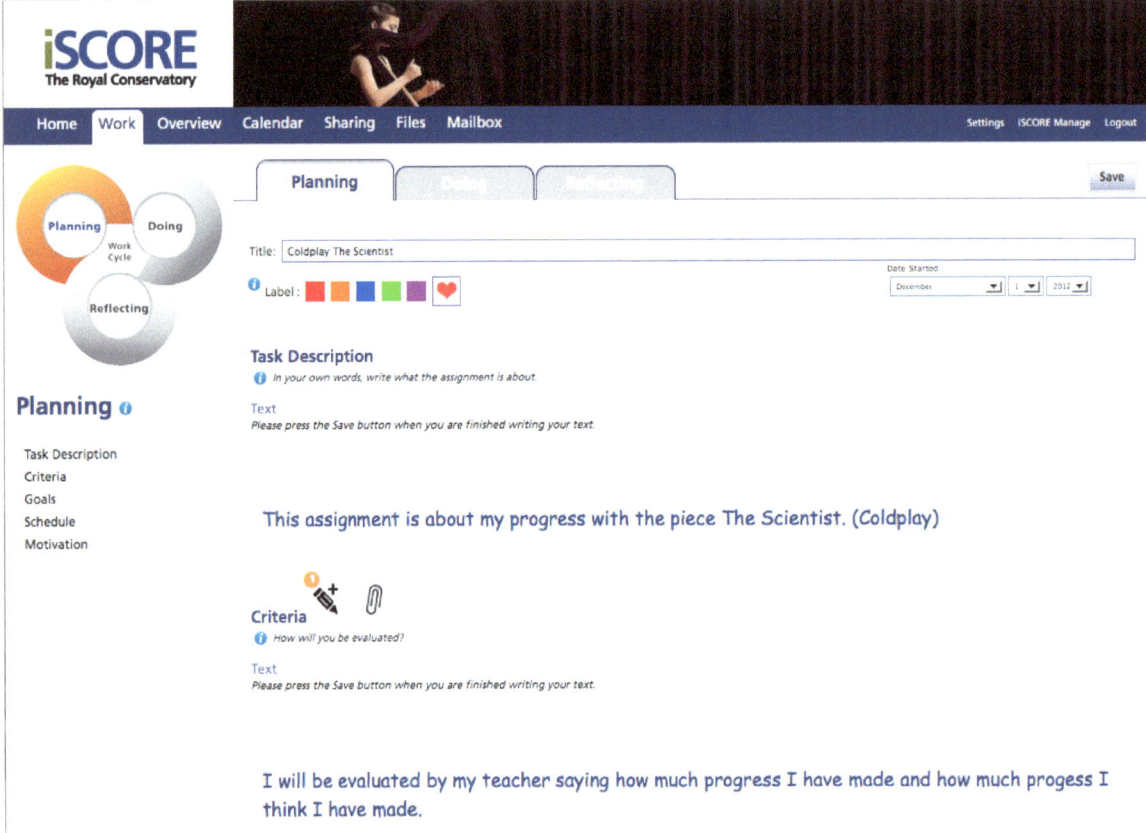

Student Exemplars

Title: Coldplay The Scientist

Self-Evaluation

How did you do? Look at the goals and criteria you set for this task. Compare the result of your efforts to your intentions and goals.

Text
Please press the Save button when you are finished writing your text.

I think I did quite well but still a little patchy.

+ Need help? Answer these:

Cause

What are the reasons for this outcome?
Did your result match your intentions? What are the reasons for this outcome?

Text
Please press the Save button when you are finished writing your text.

I think I got it pretty smooth because I played it many times through.

Satisfaction

Overall, how satisfied are you with your performance?

least [====   ] most

Lessons Learned

What can you do differently next time you approach a similar task? What are the lessons you will take away from this about yourself as a learner?

Text
Please press the Save button when you are finished writing your text.

I think maybe I could practice a little more.

Using iSCORE to Compose: *Crescent*

This exemplar illustrates the work of an intermediate student who used iSCORE to compose a piece, titled *Crescent.* The planning and reflecting phases are shown here.

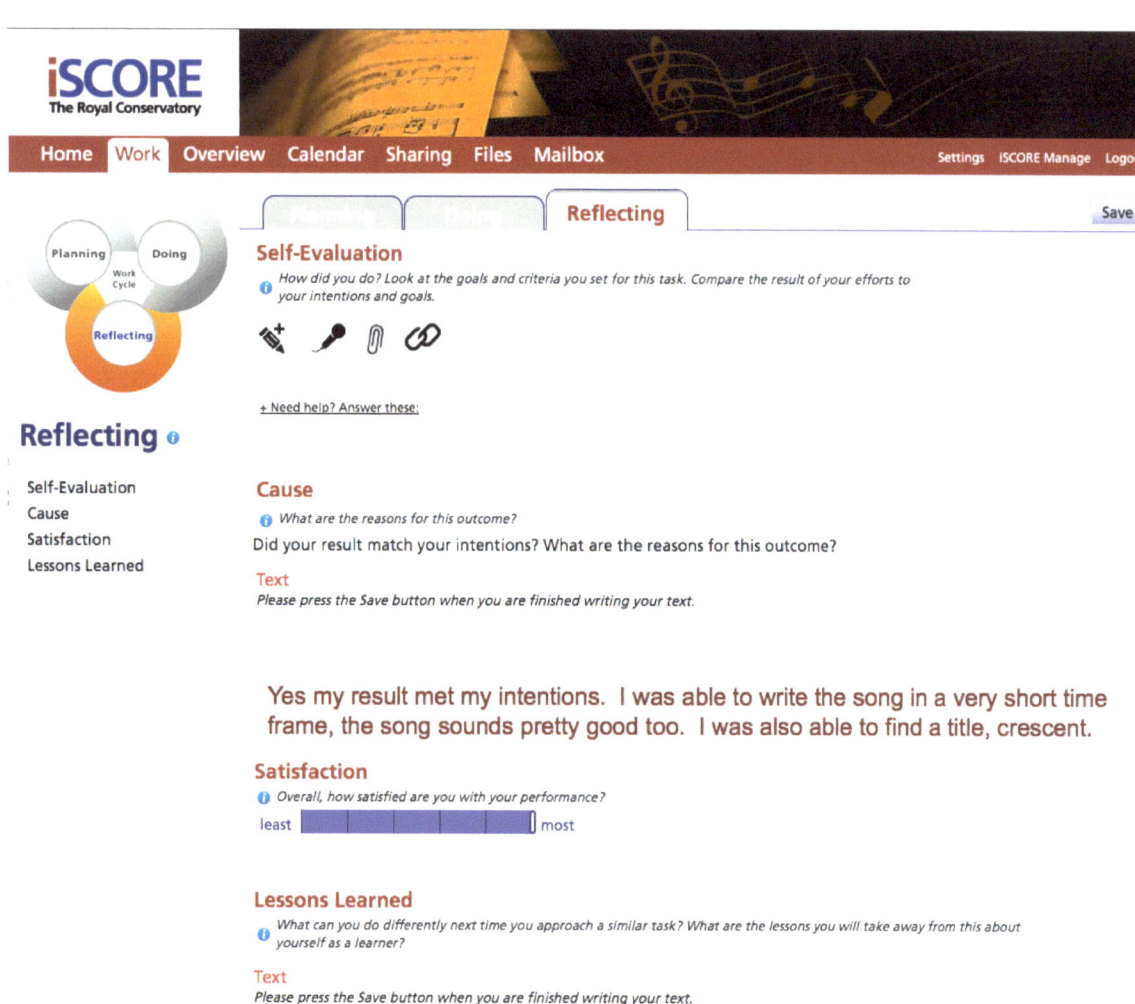

Using iSCORE for a Quick Study: *Bagatelle*

This exemplar shows how a student, preparing for the local music festival's "quick study" class, used iSCORE to help him meet his goal of learning a Grade 8 level piece in 48 hours. Instead of seeing the screen shots, what you see here is the exported file. Exported files are useful when students want to show their completed work. However, it is not possible to access the audio or video recordings once a work is exported. So we have used screen shots to illustrate the Doing phase of the self-regulation cycle.

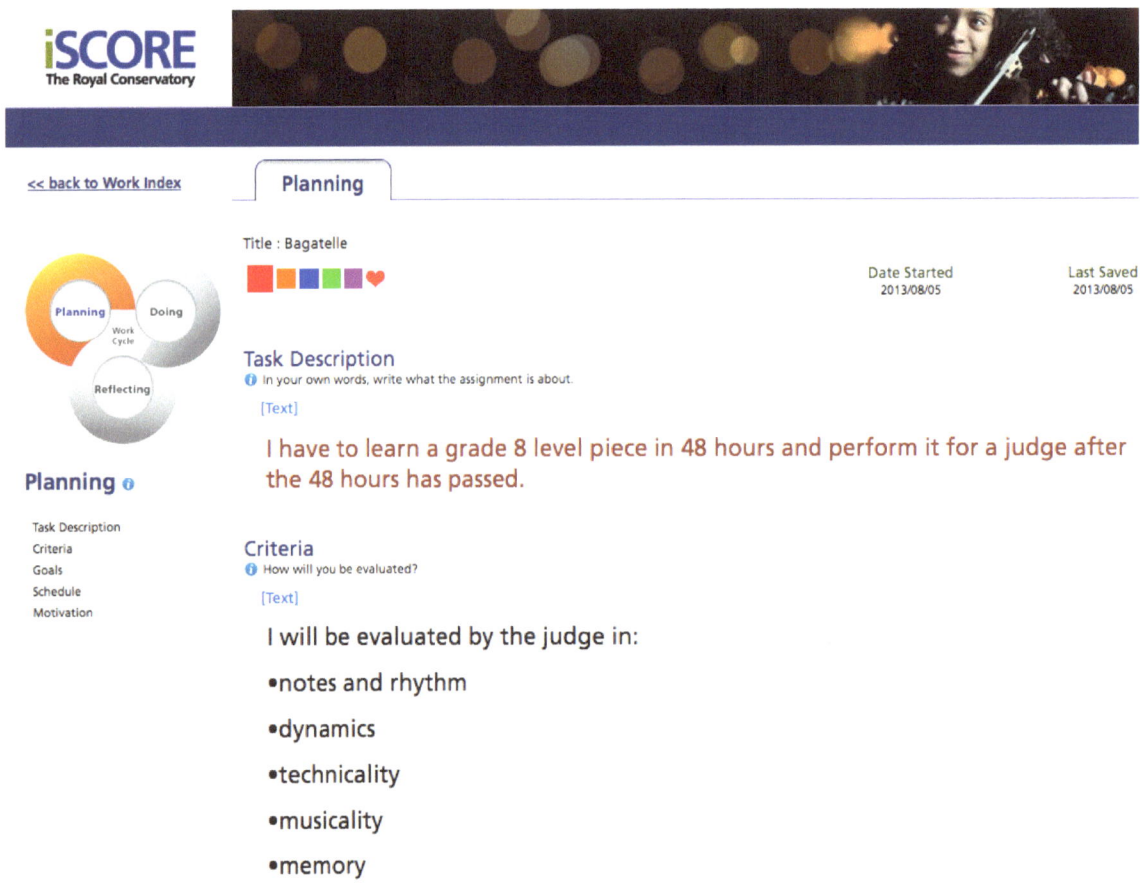

This serves as an example of a task goal with supporting strategies as it appears when the file has been exported. In learning the *Bagatelle*, the student had three separate task goals, with a number of overlapping strategies (learn notes, check rhythm, and dynamics).

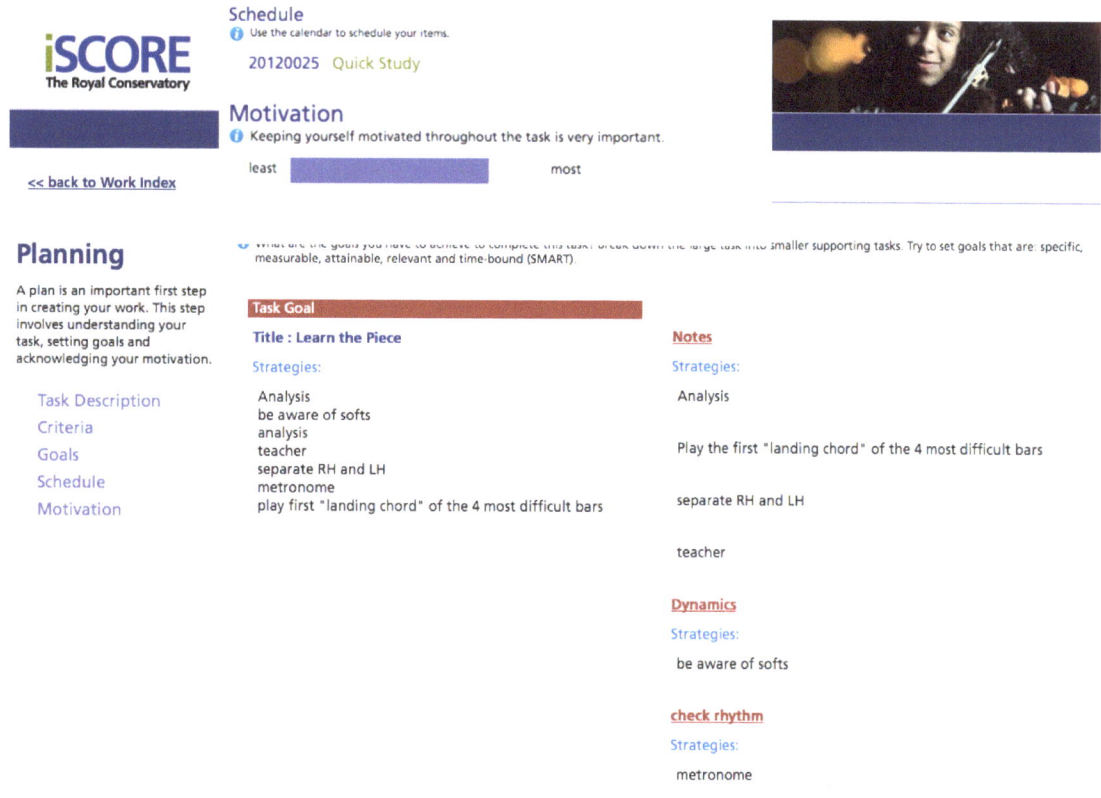

This shows two of the student's video recordings in annotated form. They are from the portfolio itself, not the export page, as work on the Doing tab *does not export*.

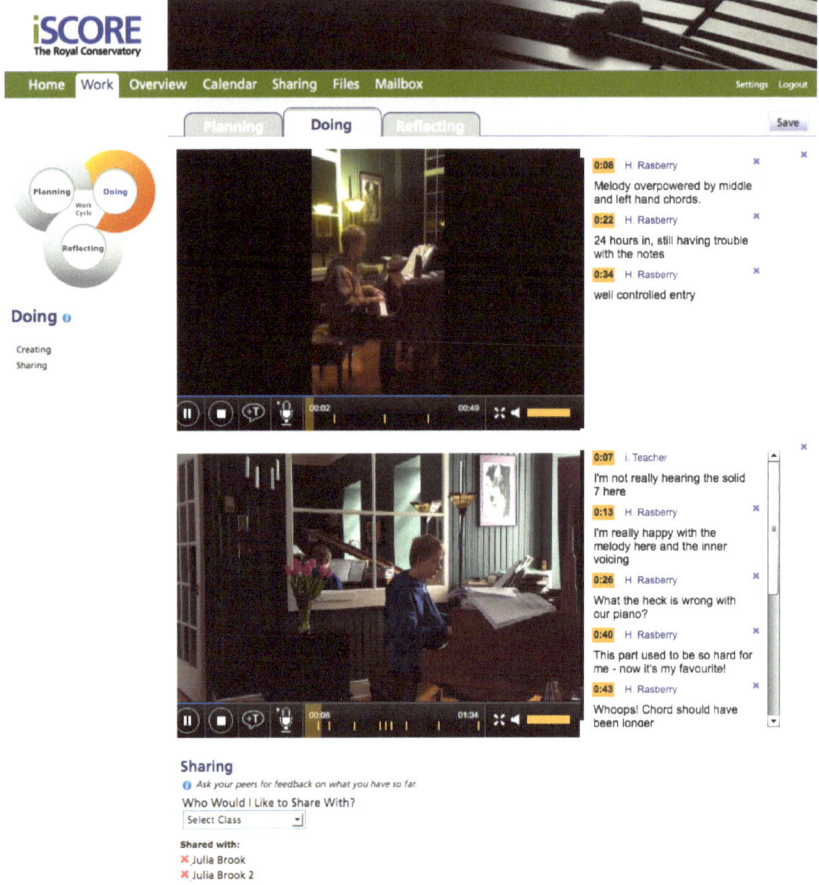

These final pages show examples of the student's reflections, with some as exported pages and others as screen shots from the Reflecting tab.

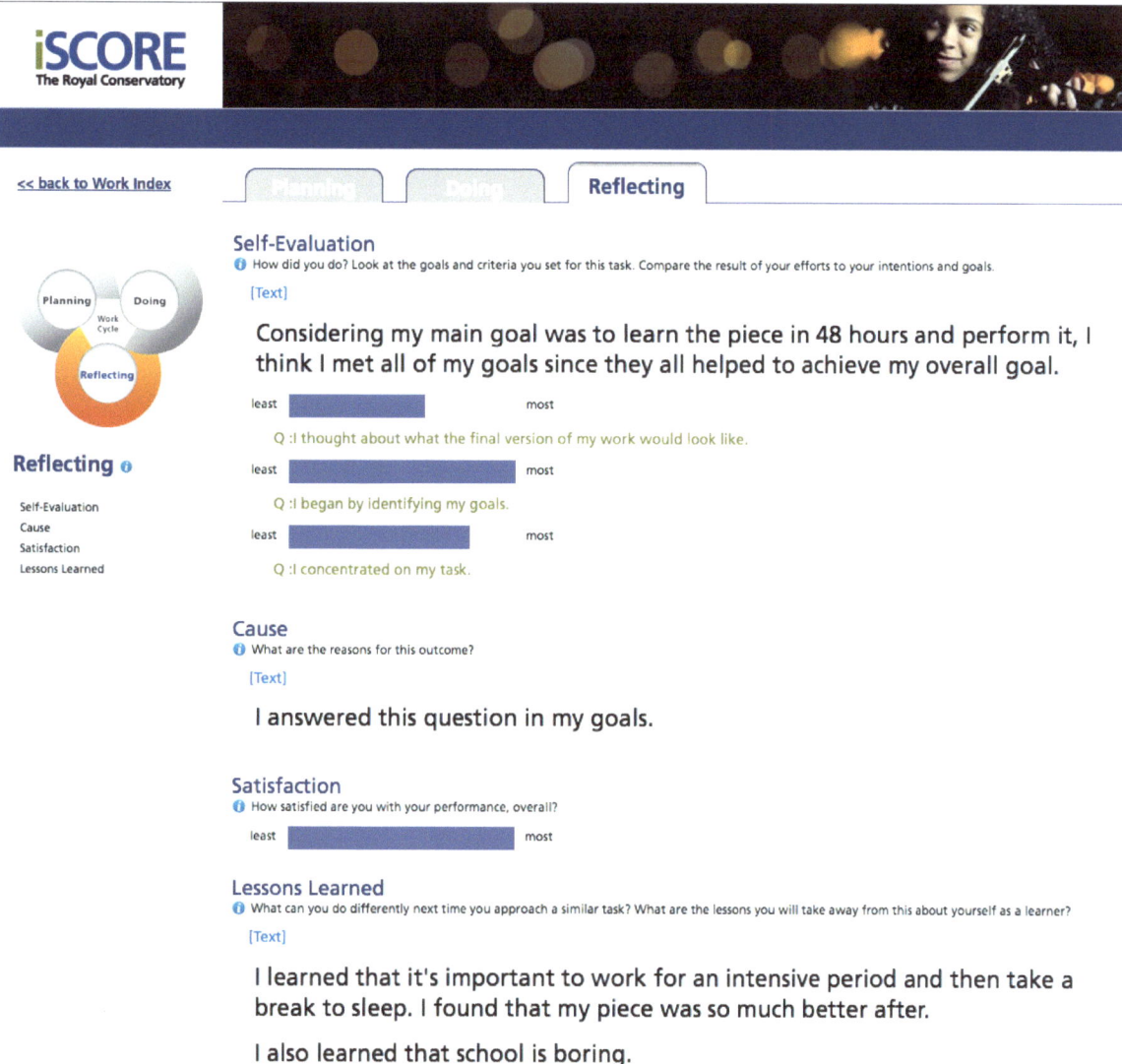

On the following two pages, screen shots from the actual portfolio (not the exported files) appear, showing more detail about the student's reflections.

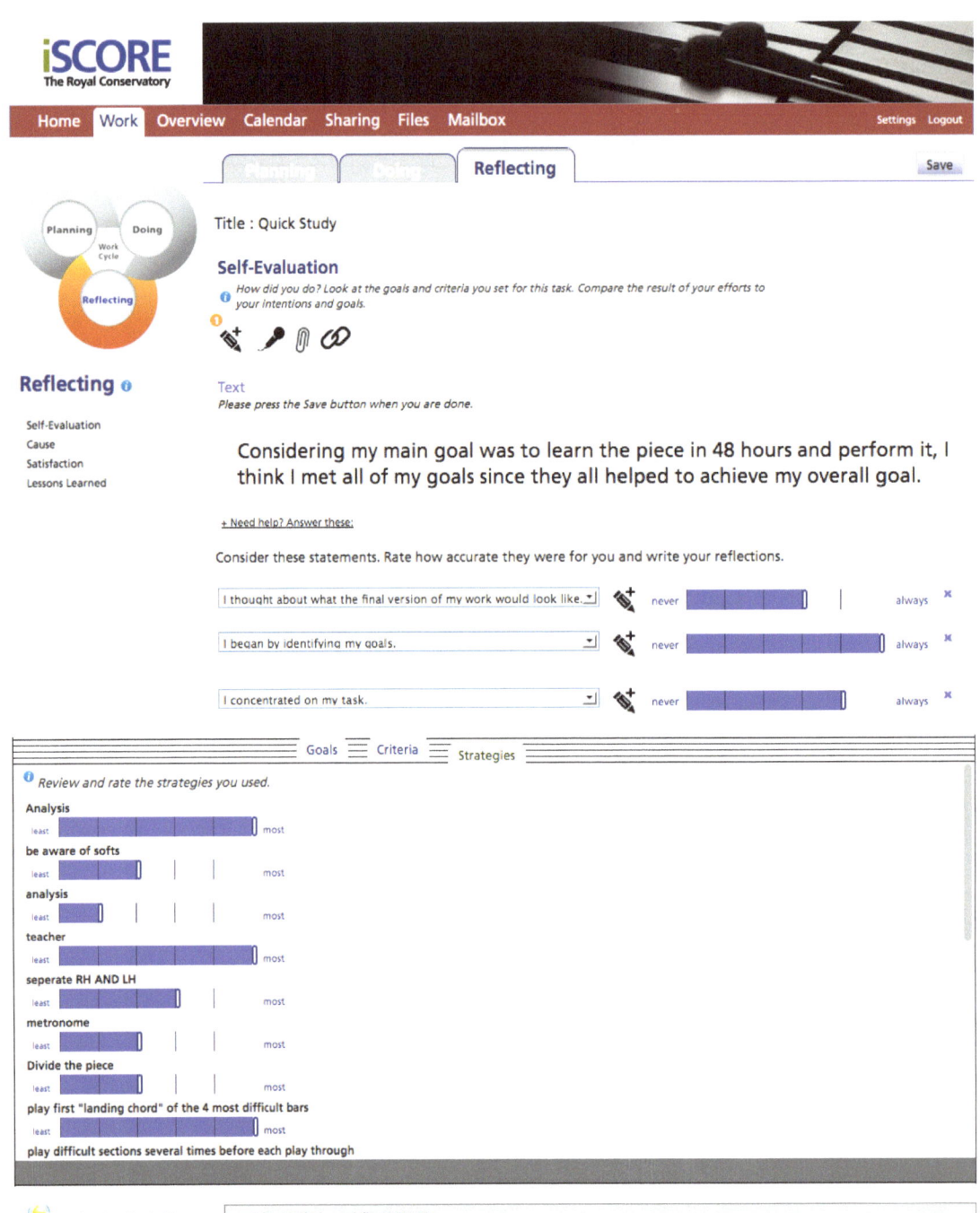

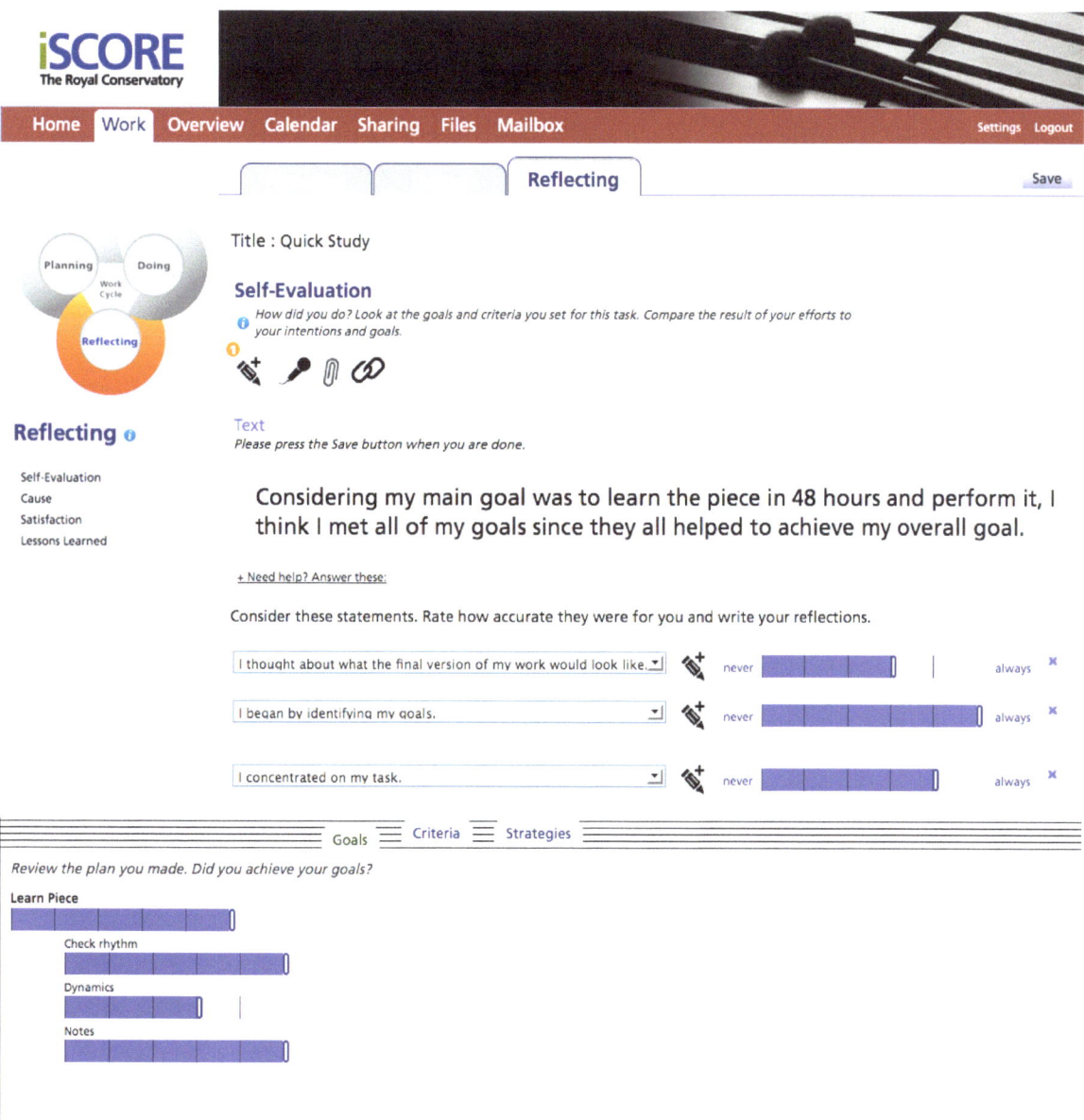

ACKNOWLEDGEMENTS

The design of iSCORE was based on the evidence-based ePEARL software, as well as input from RCM faculty and staff, independent music teachers, colleagues, music students, and parents. Our team:

Management: Philip Abrami (Director, CSLP, Concordia University), Angela Elster (Vice-President Academic, The Royal Conservatory [RCM]), and Rena Upitis (Professor, Queen's University)

Developers: Catherine LeBel (Creative Director, CSLP), Jonathan Castonguay-Harding (CSLP), Andrew Gardner (CSLP), J. J. Hwang (CSLP), Steven Kanellopoulos-Kanellos (CSLP), Sebastien Rainville (CSLP), and Mimi Zhou (CSLP)

Instructional Designers: Einat Idan (CSLP) and Anne Wade (CSLP)

Researchers: Philip Abrami (CSLP), Wynnpaul Varela (CSLP), Julia Brook (Queen's), Scott Hughes (Queen's), Meagan Troop (Queen's), Serena Manson (Queen's), Karen Boese (Queen's), and Rena Upitis (Queen's)

Videographer: Renee Jackson (CSLP)

Field Testers and Teacher Advisors: Marie Anderson, Julia Brook, Angela Chan, Joseph Ferretti, Elaine Lau, Heidi Saario, Julia Fountain, Meagan Troop, and Anne Wade

RCM Advisors and Developers: Gerry Dimnik, Anita Hardeman, Laura Johnson, Janet Lopinski, Jennifer Snow

Translator: Marie-Claude Plourde, *Binôme*

Special thanks to the following people: Brian Bell (RCM), Jane Blake (RCM), Evelyne Cyphiot (CSLP), Patricia Yetman (CSLP), Lyse Larose (Concordia), Keira Enneson Park (RCM), Donna Takacs (RCM), and Jane Willms (Queen's).

© 2011—Version 1.0. All rights reserved. The software may not be used without the written permission of The RCM. Not for sale or re-sale.
© 2013—Version 2.0. All rights reserved. The software may not be used without the written permission of The RCM. Not for sale or re-sale.

The development of iSCORE was supported by:

The Matthews Family

Canadian Heritage   Patrimoine canadien

iSCORE research, professional development, and knowledge mobilization is supported by:

Canada Foundation for Innovation
Fondation canadienne pour l'innovation

Wintergreen Studios Press is an independent literary press. It is affiliated with the not-for-profit educational retreat centre, Wintergreen Studios, and supports the work of Wintergreen Studios by publishing works related to education, culture, and the environment.

www.wintergreenstudios.com

www.ingramcontent.com/pod-product-compliance
Lightning Source LLC
Chambersburg PA
CBHW041535220426
43663CB00002B/44